COLLECTION FALL/WINTER 1992/93. *"PUTTI" BY POP SWATCH*

GO AHEAD

PATRONS
OF THE ENTERTAINMENT ARTISTES' BENEVOLENT FUND

Her Majesty Queen Elizabeth II

Pictured above with HRH Prince Phillip, being escorted into the Royal Box by Lord Delfont,
for the start of an LWT organised Royal Variety Performance.

Her Majesty Queen Elizabeth The Queen Mother

Pictured below meeting cast members -
Una Stubbs, Jan Francis & Esther Rantzen - after a BBC organised Royal Variety Performance.

Foreword

by
Lord Delfont
Life President
of The E.A.B.F.

Having been associated with the Entertainment Artistes' Benevolent Fund now for over 35 years and having presented the Royal Variety Performance as well as being the Life President of this wonderful organisation, I wish Charterhouse Publications every success in their magnificent effort to put in book form a history of the Fund.

The Fund has existed since 1907 to assist variety artistes initially, who had fallen on hard times either through age or ill health and to provide financial help for those unfortunate members of our profession.

Brinsworth House was purchased in 1911 to provide a home for members of the variety profession who could no longer sustain themselves in their own homes, and in some cases, of course, incoming residents to Brinsworth did not even have their own homes but lived in either digs, which was common in those days, or small hotels. In later years the Fund encompassed not only members of the variety side of our business but also members of the circus, television and all forms of light entertainment.

In 1990, at a cost of over £500,000, a new nursing wing was established at Brinsworth House, thus enabling residents who were taken ill to no longer have to leave their home and go into hospital, but to remain at Brinsworth to be nursed and cared for in what was to become known as The Leslie Grade Wing. It gave me great personal pleasure that my brother was honoured in this way and that Her Majesty Queen Elizabeth The Queen Mother personally came to Brinsworth House to officiate the opening, which took place on 5th April 1990.

The Royal Family have been great stalwarts of the Fund since its original conception and the cornerstone of the Fund's financial structure is the Royal Variety Performance which the Royal Family have supported now for over 65 years. With the charity needing in the region of £1 million per year to look after the 36 residents at Brinsworth House and provide aid for the 300 beneficiaries that are scattered around the country, every £1 that is donated to the Fund is badly needed. So your contribution to help the Fund by purchasing this fine publication is gratefully received, and our thanks are extended to you for your support for this very worthy cause.

Your contribution today is helping the people who have entertained you and your families in the past.

CREDITS

EDITOR
Peter Hepple

ART DIRECTOR
Gary Lysandrou

**PRODUCTION DIRECTOR
& EDITORIAL CO-ORDINATOR**
Nancy Menhinick

PRODUCTION ASSISTANT
Faith Yerkes

PUBLISHER
George Andrews

SALES EXECUTIVES
David Fosk
Geoffrey Dobson
Don Torrence
Sharon Stalker
Lucy James

PUBLISHED FOR THE E.A.B.F.
by Charterhouse Publications Ltd
Directa House
114-118 Kingsland Road
London E2 8DP
Tel: 071-739 1803
Fax: 071-613 3073

REPRODUCTION
Data Layout
071 403 8106

PRINTERS
Stephens & George
0685 388888

Acknowledgements

Without the help of all our authors, their agents and publicists, this book would not have been possible. Their time and effort is appreciated and we thank everyone involved in this project. Our grateful thanks also go to all those who supplied pictures and illustrations as listed below.

Copyright for pictures remain with the following:

BBC Photo Library
Sue Boorman
Chorley and Handford
Clifford Elson Publicity Ltd.
Mike Craig
Stanley Dallas
Lord Delfont
Ken Dodd
Peter Elliott
Valerie Garland
George Bartram Associates
Roy Hudd
David Jamieson, King Pole Magazine published by Circus Friends Assoc.
LWT Press Stills Library
Mander & Mitchenson
Jack Seaton
Kay Smart
Don Smoothey
Bert Weedon
Alan Whitehead, The London Palladium

Front cover illustration
copyright of Andy Tucker,
produced by him specially
for That's Entertainment.

Background picture
to this page, from a
1953 variety programme,
courtesy of Roy Hudd.

CONTENTS

Foreword - by Lord Delfont   3

Introduction - by Peter Elliott   6

A Short History of Variety - by Roy Hudd   12

My Silver Ghosts (Variety on Film) - by Jimmy Perry   24

Variety on Stage - by Peter Hepple   32

Variety on Radio - by Mike Craig   40

The BBC and Variety - by Yvonne Littlewood   46

The Future of Variety on Television - John Kaye Cooper, LWT   58

Animal Training - by Sue Boorman   67

The Many Faces of Russ Abbott (interview)   72

Ode to Frank - by Barry Cryer   82

From the Shirrell Brothers to Cannon and Ball (interview)   84

Dick Emery - An Appreciation by Peter Elliott   88

Billy Dainty - An Appreciation by Len Lowe   92

The Life and Times of Jim Davidson (interview)   96

Les Dawson - An Appreciation - by John Smerin   106

A Day in the Life of an Agent - by Stanley Dallas   112

Ken Dodd - Born to Entertain (interview)   116

Tommy Trinder - by Jack Seaton   122

Ben Warriss - A Life on the Boards (interview)   134

Arthur Askey - by Mike Craig   140

The London Palladium - Louis Benjamin (interview)   146

A Life in the Circus - by Kay Smart   151

British Music Hall Society - by J.O. Blake   157

The Water Rats - by King Rat Bert Weedon   162

The Grand Order of Lady Ratlings - by Dorita Chester   166

The Vaudeville Golfing Society - by Alf Pearson   168

Royal Variety Performance - by Yvonne Littlewood   170

Introduction

by
Peter Elliott
Executive Administrator
of The E.A.B.F.

As the Executive Administrator of this wonderful charity, and having spent my whole working life in the the theatrical profession, it gives me constant joy and personal satisfaction to see, on a daily basis, the wonderful work that is being done at Brinsworth House, to enhance the lives of members of our profession who have become members of our family. The constant care that is administered by our nursing staff, care assistants, cooks, cleaners, gardeners, administrative staff and all connected with the charity is quite remarkable. Their welfare is the prime object of the Fund's existence, although the beneficiaries who are living in their own homes, but still seeking and getting financial assistance from us, are also of prime importance. Visits are made and phone calls are taken from people in need and every effort is made to make life easier for those less fortunate than ourselves.

This publication will hopefully enhance the coffers of the Fund, which in turn will be spent on the people that I have mentioned. So, many thanks for supporting us and I hope you enjoy the articles which friends of the EABF have sweated over for love not money! We thank them all for their love and support.

For those of you who know nothing about Brinsworth House and the EABF, I hope the following three pages will be enlightening.

Brinsworth House

A beautiful home in a tranquil setting, virtually in the middle of Twickenham, Brinsworth House accommodates some 36 residents, each with his or her own room complete with colour television, and constant care from a staff under the direction and guidance of the Fund's Senior Nursing Officer.

Brinsworth residents may be fee-paying, or DSS-supported.

Since acquiring Brinsworth House in 1911, the Fund has sought continually to improve the amenities. A major development occurred in 1976 when Her Majesty Queen Elizabeth The Queen Mother opened a new £250,000 wing, making possible the transition from dormitory accommodation to single rooms.

More recently, in April 1990, Her Majesty Queen Elizabeth The Queen Mother opened the new £500,000 Leslie Grade wing - a nursing unit which allows residents who are taken ill the luxury of being medically treated 'at home' rather than having to go to hospital. The provision of this wing was made possible by the leadership of the Fund's Life President, Lord Delfont, together with the continued generosity of the Grand Order of Water Rats and many other show business organisations and individuals.

7

The E. A. B. F.

Since its inception in the early years of this century, the Entertainment Artistes' Benevolent Fund has been caring unstintingly for retired, elderly and needy members of the theatrical profession, working in light entertainment, circus, or television - or dependants of an artiste in this category.

This help is applied in two ways, in the maintenance of Brinsworth House, and as 'Samaritan' aid in the form of direct financial assistance to needy artistes nationwide. These finances help to pay for fuel bills, winter clothing, nursing home fees, television rentals and license fees, and funeral costs.

The Fund is very conscious of the incalculable enhancement that the Royal Patronage confers upon its status. This gracious patronage is the cornerstone upon which the Fund's success has been built, while the presence in the Royal Box of Their Majesties The Queen or The Queen Mother at the Royal Variety Performances makes the occasions what they are, thus enabling the Fund to continue its humanitarian work.

History

The Fund originated during one of the regular meetings of the Music Hall Artistes' Railway Association in 1908, where a member, Joe O'Gorman, conscious of the hardships that could befall elderly or infirm artistes in an insecure profession, proposed that a levy be charged on the Association's annual subscription, and that the funds so raised should be used to create a financial base for a benevolent fund.

Joe O'Gorman's suggestion was enthusiastically adopted by fellow-member Joe Elvin, who was not only to become the Fund's first President but also contributed £500 of his own.

By 1911 Joe O'Gorman and Joe Elvin, the twin architects of the Fund, had sufficient reserves to consider the acquisition of a residential home for elderly, retired or infirm Music Hall artistes. They found Brinsworth House in Twickenham. The cost: £2,500. The Fund put down £1,000 and raised the remaining £1,500 on mortgage. Enter W.H. McCarthy, Secretary of the Fund, with the proposal that a Membership of the Noble Order of 600 be created, with a subscription of £2.10s. (£2.50) per head. It succeeded. By 1913 the mortgage was paid off and the Fund had the ownership and freehold of Brinsworth House.

The premise of pure classic design is an uncompromising marriage of technology and style, looks and performance.

The pinnacle of such a blend is Celestion's Units range of affordable stand/bookshelf and floor-standing speakers.

Designed to suit the budget or more sophisticated music system, the range is enhanced by the new Celestion 1, a masterpiece of loud speaker engineering, the Celestion 15, a tall, slim yet immensely powerful floor standing column and the Celestion CS 135, an exceptional subwoofer designed to provide a deep yet subtle extended bass to the Celestion 1,3 and 5 speakers.

Performance,technology and style in one unique range.

Only from Celestion.

1 • 3 • 5 • 7 • 9 • 11 • 15 • CS135

The Fund Today

The largest single annual source of the Fund's income today are the proceeds of the Royal Variety Performance, which has been presented and arranged in aid of the Fund since 1921. For this event, the principal artistes all give their time and talents entirely free of charge. Television broadcast rights in the United Kingdom and overseas - negotiated by the Fund's Life President, Lord Delfont, in 1962 and 1971 respectively - enhance the proceeds of the event still further.

Every year, the Fund also puts on shows in conjunction with local charitable organisations. From Royal Galas at Windsor to Variety shows in theatres large and small around the country, these events raise many thousands of pounds for the benefit of the various charities, as well as for the Entertainment Artistes' Benevolent Fund itself.

These activities, together with income from donations, life subscriptions and covenants, enable the Fund to run and maintain Brinsworth House, and to continue its Samaritan support for elderly artistes around the country. Together, these residential and pastoral commitments consume over £300,000 per annum.

Ivor

Spencer

Ivor Spencer, the doyen of Toastmasters, has officiated at over 1000 Royal events at home and abroad during his 37 years in the profession.

This most famous of toastmasters, Founder & Life President of the Guild of Professional Toastmasters, is also a much sought after after-dinner speaker and banquet and conference organiser.

When Ivor Spencer organises an event for you, he organises everything: engaging top cabaret performers, bands, lighting, sound, catering and every detail of the event.

Comments

"... You are certainly the doyen of Toastmasters. It is a pleasure to work with you; your cheerful and reliable manner was a delight to all those present."
Dame Shirley Porter, Lord Mayor of Westminster, 5.5.1992.

"... During the past four years he has organised many successful functions at Claridge's and I have had the pleasure of welcoming students from his school to the hotel regularly. Mr. Spencer has great organising abilities and works to the highest standards."
Ronald F. Jones O.B.E. Director & General Manager, Claridge's, 27.10.88.

"... Obviously I will understand if I have to accept a substitute, although nobody can really substitute for Ivor Spencer! ..."
Donald du Parc Braham, Chairman,
Westminster Abbey Garden Party Joint Function Cttee, 30.3.92.

"... During my time as Chairman, I always recognised the very professional skill that you have shown in carrying through your duties as a master of ceremonies."
W.A. Craddock, Deputy Chairman, Harrods, 17.11.88.

Principal of the Ivor Spencer School for Professional Toastmasters
Sole Agent for Town Criers of England

IVOR SPENCER
GUILD OF PROFESSIONAL TOASTMASTERS
12 LITTLE BORNES
ALLEYN PARK, DULWICH SE21 8SE

Tel: 081-670 5585 / 081-670 8424   Fax: 081-670 0055   Car Phone 0860 313835

A SHORT HISTORY OF VARIETY

BY ROY HUDD

Roy Hudd learned his craft in the late fifties, the last days of concert party and variety. His stage career has included everything from pantomime, variety, musicals, and farce to Shakespeare and Stoppard.

His television work has included 'Not So Much a Programme More a Way of Life', 'The Maladjusted Busker', 'The Illustrated Weekly Hudd', 'Comedy Tonight', 'The 607080 Show', 'Movie Memories', 'Halls of Fame', 'The Puppet Man', 'Hometown,' a series of 'What's My Line?' and numerous guest spots.

His radio career started in the sixties with 'Worker's Playtime' and has, for the last seventeen years, been crowned with BBC Radio Two's 'The News Huddlines'. Practically every top comedy writer has cut his or her teeth on the show which has taken every radio trophy at home and abroad.

Roy Hudd the writer emerged in the late seventies. His book on his great love 'Music Hall' is now a collector's item and his stage shows have included Roy Hudd's very own 'Music Hall', 'Just a Verse and Chorus', numerous pantomimes and 'Underneath the Arches', for which he won the Best Actor in a Musical Award from the Society of West End Theatres.

In 1989 he was elected King Rat in the centenary year of the show business organisation, The Grand Order of Water Rats.

In 1991 he received the Sony Gold Award for "Outstanding contribution to radio over many years" and the LWT Comedy Award for "lifetime achievement in radio comedy". The summer was spent at The Open Air Theatre, Regents Park collecting "rave" National reviews playing Bottom in 'A Midsummer Night's Dream'. The Autumn meant a nationwide tour with his one man music hall show - not an empty seat at any performance! - and recording the 300th edition of 'The News Huddlines' with, of course, the wonderful June Whitfield. Pantomime was at the Theatre Royal, Plymouth, with his 'Babes in the Wood'. The show broke every box office record.

1992 has included more "Huddlines", the new Dennis Potter series for Channel Four, 'Lipstick on Your Collar', and another Nationwide tour with his 'Very Own Music Hall'.

This year's panto will be his third at the New Theatre, Cardiff. He first appeared here as one of the Broker's Men in the early sixties with Clarkson Rose and the last time in 1979 with Wyn Calvin in 'Dick Whittington'.

Roy writes a regular monthly column for 'Yours' magazine and is President of The British Music Hall Society.

Variety is dead! So what's new. People have been saying it since Will Kemp was given the elbow by William Shakespeare.

They said it when Charles Morton, "The Father of the Music Halls", daringly opened the doors of his establishment, in the 1850's, to women. They said it in 1892 when Edison invented the phonograph and again in 1896 when moving pictures were first shown.

In 1912 a band called the American Ragtime Octette appeared, in variety, at the London Hippodrome. The purists threw up their hands and declared "It's all over," while George Robey had them thrown off the bill! In the 1950's the great Max Miller used to say "When I'm dead and gone the game's finished!"

In the seventies the closing of the giant clubs like Batley and Wakefield signalled the end yet again and the announcement by a television mogul in the '80s that "Variety is finished" seemed to be the final nail in the coffin. But it wasn't you know.

Today, for all the excesses of those whose sole purpose seems to be to shock, it is still alive. In fact more alive than it's been for many years. The art of Variety is the art of the live performer, the ability to be able to involve your audience. Always was and always will be. As television gets more bland and predictable more and more people, young and old, are getting out and about and looking for the 'live' experience. That experience is Variety's trump card.

So, having hopefully convinced you that Variety is still alive, I get down to my brief. "Write a history of Variety in three thousand words" said the publisher. Impossible.

So many people have written great learned tomes on the subject and still there are glaring gaps. I can only skate over the surface for you and hope that you'll pop into your library and find some of the M. Wilson Disher, W. Macqueen Pope and Mander and Mitchenson belting books on the great British invention - Variety. Oh and I mustn't forget the very best book on Variety, "A Funny Way To Be A Hero", by John Fisher.

The roots of Variety do go back to Shakespeare's time and before. At every country fair there were always 'turns' to entertain. Comic singers, jugglers, acrobats and performing animals. Variety bills in fact. But I want to concentrate on the last one hundred and fifty years.

This was the golden period when two great slices of what we now call Light Entertainment happened. Music Hall and Variety. One blended into the other so subtly that it is difficult to know when one began and the other ended. They are different though and for the purposes of this quick peek let's assume that Music Hall ran roughly from around the mid-eighteen hundreds to just before the First World War and from then on it was called Variety.

It is fairly easy to distinguish between Music Hall and Variety. You can fairly say that Music Hall was an entertainment in a large eating and drinking type place, with the acts introduced by a Chairman, and Variety was a non-stop parade of performers in a theatre usually introduced to the audience by an illuminated number (situated on the proscenium arch) which corresponded to the one next to their name in a printed programme.

There are very few, if any, people alive today who actually saw Music Hall but the flavour of it is pretty well documented so we can see how the Variety industry grew from very humble beginnings.

The seventeenth century saw the first stirrings of Music Hall with shows presented, both indoors and alfresco, in the Pleasure Gardens (today we have Euro Disney and Alton Towers). Sadler's Wells had a famous public garden and a contemporary report from 1699 describes a visit to a music 'house' there. The writer tells, in verse, how he and his companion -

Having refreshed ourselves after our walk
Looked o'er the gallery like the rest of the folk.

He then describes the occupants of the ground floor - the pit.

Where butchers and bailiffs and such sort of fellows
Were mixed with a vermin trained up to the gallows.

The first 'turn' comes on to the platform

With hands on her belly, she open'd her throat
And silenced the noise with her musical note.
The guests were all hush and attention was given
The listening mob thought themselves in a Heaven!
And the ravishing song which she sung? you would
                                                    know
It was "Rub, rub, rub; rub, rub, rub; in and out ho."

Good clean stuff for the kiddies aye! This gives you some idea of the sophisticated stuff the Pleasure Garden audiences enjoyed. Mind you we've got one or two today who would have been more than at home. The poem continues:

As soon as her sweet modest ditty was done
She withdrew from the platform as chaste as a Nun
The butchers were so pleased with her warbling strain
That they cheered her and clapped her
All round for her pain!

The rest of the piece describes what is in effect a Music hall programme of a hundred and fifty years later. A fiddler, a sword swallower and a top of the bill comedian who ...

Makes his whole person as good as a Farce.

I omit the line that rhymed with it!

The Pleasure Garden entertainments would have been by professional performers but by the mid-eighteenth century semi-amateur, all-male, sing-songs had become very popular. They called these 'dos' Harmonic Meetings but they were really just excuses for blokes to have a boozy night out down the local.

At these evenings the host, usually the landlord of the pub where the meetings happened, would take the chair and then persuade all present to do something to entertain their fellow roisterers. It could be a story, a song, a balancing trick or an imitation. Not unlike the Christmas get-togethers we had at home when I was a kid. The only difference was in the pubs a refusal to oblige meant paying a forfeit - like drinking a pint of salt water!

Gradually these free and easy evenings became more professional - when the organizers realised more people turned up to buy their booze when certain people promised to perform. They began to pay the more popular ones. I'd have loved to have seen some of them. George Alexander Stevens, in 1763, described the 'stars':

One plays with a rolling pin upon a salt box, another grunts like a hog while a third makes his teeth chatter like a monkey.

And you thought heavy metal was new!

By the early nineteenth century we were very near to authentic Music Hall. Paid performers entertaining in huge pubs.

Around this time the brewers started to add on to their pubs special buildings to accommodate the huge crowds that used to turn up. They called these places "Halls of Music" - Music Halls. One such place "The Grecian Saloon", built on to "The Eagle" pub in the City Road, has been immortalised in the nursery rhyme:

Up and down the City Road
In and out of "The Eagle"
That's the way the money goes
Pop! Goes the weasel

The very first purpose built Hall was supposed to be "The Surrey", attached to "The

The Holborn Empire claims to be London's real Music Hall but the early Music Halls were attached to public houses.

Grapes" pub in Southwark Bridge Road, but the most famous was "The Canterbury Music Hall", attached to "The Canterbury Arms" in the Westminster Bridge Road.

It was the brainchild of the most important man in the history of Music Hall, Charles Morton. He was a publican who'd always staged simple sing-songs in his houses but "The Canterbury" was a far cry from these. It was posh by any yardstick, with lots of plush and chandeliers.

Eventually it featured an art gallery and could accommodate over fifteen hundred people. Morton employed the best performers of the day and upped their money to astronomical heights. George Leybourne, the original "Champagne Charlie", earned over a hundred pounds a week there. How much was that in the 1800's? He was worth it. He put "bums on seats" and that then, as today, was what popular entertainment was all about.

George Leybourne had a song called "The Man On The Flying Trapeze". It was based on the exploits of another Music Hall star, a Frenchman who caused a sensation by "flying" over the heads of the eaters and drinkers. He gave his name to the 'all in one' outfit dancers still wear to rehearse in. He was Monsieur Leotard.

One little side track re: Charles Morton. At the age of seventy four he was asked to save The English Opera House. He did, by making it a Music Hall. The theatre still stands as The Palace in Shaftesbury Avenue. "Thank you Mr. Morton," says Sir Andrew Lloyd Webber.

The Halls grew bigger and more elaborate and produced names that are still spoken of in awe today. Dan Leno, Marie Lloyd,

DON'T LISTEN TO IT. LIVE IT.

Kenwood Hi-Fi. One step closer to the total experience. For people who demand more from life than background music.

Kenwood M26:1-bit CD, turntable, Presence mode graphic equaliser, twin auto reverse cassette, tuner and 35 watts per channel.

Part of a range of midi Hi-Fi systems from around £449 to £1,049. For brochure and nearest dealer, phone free on 0800 100110.

KENWOOD
HOME Hi-Fi ■ CAR Hi-Fi
moved by music

Albert Chevalier, Vesta Tilley, Gus Elen, Little Tich, Eugene Stratton, Harry Champion, George Robey and Harry Lauder (The first Music Hall performer to be knighted).

The list is endless and is far better documented elsewhere, as are the immortal songs they gave us. They were all larger than life personalities who had the indispensable gift of being able to control huge, hard-drinking audiences but these so called "good old days" were soon to come to an end.

The Edwardian audiences wanted 'family' amusement and popular entertainment had to give the punters what they wanted. The Music Hall died with the abandonment of drinking in the auditorium and the Chairman as host.

As Morton had been "The Father of the Halls" so Sir Oswald Stoll sired Variety. He took the vulgarity away and made Variety acceptable. Many people also say he took away the red-blooded, subversive anarchy too. He was an odd sort of chap to promote Variety.

From what I've learnt Sir Oswald was a stuffy, rather prissy, puritanical Mrs. Grundy yet he had been in charge of his family's Music Hall, The Pantheon in Liverpool, at the age of fourteen. He became Chairman and Managing Director of Moss Empires,

built Variety theatres all over the country, and the London Coliseum.

He had wanted for some time to build a theatre in London and chose the site for the Coliseum by making notes of the places where most people passed. He was a shrewd businessman indeed. He put his

One of Sir Oswald Stoll's 'posh' variety bills.

own mother in charge of the box office! He had a notice in every one of the dressing rooms of his theatres. "Do not ask for complimentary tickets. If your friends won't pay to see you, who will!"

His Variety bills, especially at the Coliseum, were noted for their refinement. No trace of what George Robey called "honest vulgarity" there. He raised the acceptability of popular entertainment to such a degree that Sarah Bernhardt, Ellen Terry and the Diaghilev Ballet all appeared as 'turns' at the Coliseum. With much behind the scenes string pulling by his partner Sir Edward Moss, he enabled the first Royal Command Performance to take place in 1912. Stoll said of this gentrifying of what was, and always should be, the entertainment of the man in the street, "The Cinderella of the Arts has gone to the Ball." Alas midnight was to come far too soon. Within fifty years there wouldn't be a single Music Hall in London and precious few outside.

The bill of the first Royal Show was a safe one. No Marie Lloyd. Unforgivable. She was the most popular Variety star of the day but thought not a dainty enough dish to set before the King. Her response? "Every performance by Marie Lloyd is a Command Performance - by command of the British public!" Take that Ossie!

But Variety was doing well in the twenties. There were plenty of good honestly vulgar performers around, packing 'em out, and every city and town had its own Variety Theatre.

In the thirties things were still good. There were performers with the attack and originality of the early stars who could bring the magic of live entertainment to every part of the British Isles. Will Fyffe, Billy Bennett, Gracie Fields, The Crazy Gang, Max Miller, Robb Wilton, Will Hay, Tessie O'Shea, George Formby and Tommy Trinder.

There were even, as there always had been, performers who were special to their own areas and rarely moved outside it. Frank E. Franks the Geordie, Harry Gordon and Dave Willis the Scots, Albert Modley the Yorkshireman and Jimmy O'Dea the Irishman.

The moving picture, which had originally been a novelty 'turn' in Variety, was the first serious threat to the business. Thousands of cinemas were built and suddenly a regular date at the 'flicks' was as popular as the weekly visit to the local Empire or Palace.

Then came radio. Millions of sets were purchased and, though Variety cashed in by presenting the Radio names 'live', the public had smelt they could get something for nothing and the smell didn't go away.

Actually there were very few radio 'names' who succeeded in Variety. Their personalities were intimate and all in the voice. The larger than life Variety setting wasn't, as they say, exactly their bag.

Arthur Askey told me a story of being on the bill with a well known radio singer. She had one 'hit' "I've Got A Little Dog That's Lost In A Fog". On her opening night, at the Chelsea Palace, her first song was greeted with polite applause, her second with less and, after the third a voice from the gallery, steeped in the Music Hall tradition, said "Darling! Give us the 'Dog' and p... off!"

The Great Marie Lloyd, amazingly not invited to the first Royal Command Performance.

The Second World War, as every war does, produced a shot in the arm for Variety with the influx of recently demobbed young performers, many of whom are still "top of the bill". Norman Wisdom, Max Bygraves, Harry Secombe and, until this year, the late Frankie Howerd. But there still weren't enough of them.

The great Palladium Variety bills of the '50s were perhaps the last throw of Variety as it had always been. Alas there weren't enough home-grown headliners so top American performers appeared in the star spot. Some were a big disappointment. The personalities that had seemed giant on record and in films were reduced to almost nothing in the 'live' situation. But those bills did allow some terrific British support acts to establish themselves as the true heirs of the Music Hall. Ted Ray; Wilson, Keppel and Betty; Joe Church and Jimmy Wheeler.

The late fifties were sad. That was when I came into the business! Every week another theatre closed. In desperation the promoters tried dragging out the last of the Music Hall names to front tatty revues, rock and roll melanges, freak shows and, the ultimate indignity, fly-blown nude parades. All to no avail. By now television had replaced radio and no one really wanted to leave their firesides.

The huge, luxuriously tarted-up working men's clubs looked as if they would be the salvation and they did have great success, for a time, cashing in on the television fame of performers and even producing their own stars. Little and Large, The Grumbleweeds, Ricky and Ronnie Dukes and The Black Abbots (their drummer was Russ Abbot). But, as their Variety theatre forebears had found, there just weren't

enough exciting house fillers for fifty two weeks of the year around and they too bit the dust.

So where from here? Sadly television seems to have abandoned the Variety show. I find this amazing as every year the

Royal Variety Performance gets enormous viewing figures and, in the theatres (albeit many of them soulless concrete blocks), the sort of Variety the public want to see draws good crowds.

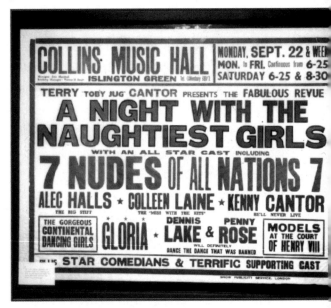

Is this the last knocking of variety?

There are still big personalities who pack 'em out without the 'help' of television. Ken Dodd, Shirley Bassey, Danny La Rue and, whether you approve of them or not, Bernard Manning and Chubby Brown.

I am a fan of the so called "alternative" comedy venues and it is there that the future lies. They are the throw back to the original Music Halls. There comics, singers and speciality acts play to vociferous, clued up and sometimes drunken audiences. Packed houses of young, and not so young, people who don't want to be spoon fed with what television decides they should

20

SHEAFFER®

Crest™ Collection
by Sheaffer

Licenced to thrill

KEN DODD · PHIL COOL · FREDDIE STARR · PAUL DANIELS

BILLY PEARCE · JASPER CARROTT · THE GRUMBLEWEEDS

JIMMY CRICKET · EDMUND HOCKRIDGE AND FAMILY · ROSE-MARIE

BOBBY KNUTT

VAL DOONICAN · THE BARRON KNIGHTS

WAYNE SLEEP · DUGGIE CHAPMAN · BEVERLEY SISTERS

LORNA LUFT · ROD HULL & EMU · CHAS 'N' DAVE

KLAUS WUNDERLICH · JOHN BRIGGS · JOHN MANN

MARTI WEBB & MARK RATTRAY · KEN GOODWIN & VICKI

BERNIE CLIFTON · KEITH HARRIS & ORVILLE

RONNE COYLES · AL MARTINO

RUSS CONWAY · BARBARA WINDSOR · THE DRIFTERS

BARRIE STACEY · ROY HUDD · JACK JONES · BIG DADDY

JETHRO · DANNY LA RUE · STAN BOARDMAN

BARBARA DICKSON · PASADENA ROOF ORCHESTRA · JANICE SUTTON STAGE SCHOOL

MAX BYGRAVES · LITTLE & LARGE

BERYL JOHNSON

CLIVE STOCK & GWEN

DAVE WILLETS

THE HARDINGS

PAT, ALAN, SOPHIE & DAVID SHEPHERD

Alan A Carr
Promotions & Publicity Manager

EMBASSY CENTRE SKEGNESS

A. Leslie Shepherd Director of Leisure & Tourism

Alan A Carr Promotions & Publicity Manager **Bob Suich** Entertainments & Amenities Manager
Steve Wattam Embassy House Manager **Betty Gough** Box Office Manager
Anne Stocks Administration Manager **Stefan Kasprzak** Chief Technical Advisor

EMBASSY CENTRE · GRAND PARADE · SKEGNESS · LINCOLNSHIRE · PE25 2UN
TELEPHONE (0754) 768444

The Oxford Theatre, one of London's two most famous houses of Variety.

have. Contrary to what so many think, all the talkers aren't just dishing out four letter words and knocking everything. They are doing what the great Variety performers have always done - giving their audience what they want. Variety is dead? Don't you believe it. It's just starting all over again.

All pictures and illustrations for this article have been supplied courtesy of Roy Hudd.

MY SILVER GHOSTS

VARIETY ON FILM

BY JIMMY PERRY, CURATOR OF THE G.O.W.R.

JIMMY PERRY was born in Barnes, London. He saw war service in the Royal Artillery in India and Burma and ran the Royal Artillery Concert Party, which later gave him the idea for the TV series "It Ain't Half Hot Mum". He studied at R.A.D.A. and started his professional career in 1950, working as a singer and comedian in Concert Party at Butlins and other summer seasons and in pantomime, revue and weekly repertory.

His first break in London was in 1952, at the Palace Theatre, in the musical "The Glorious Days", followed by several other West End musicals. In 1956 he became an actor manager, taking over the lease of the Palace Theatre, Watford, with his wife Gilda, producing weekly repertory, musicals and pantomimes. He was instrumental in the Palace becoming a Civic Theatre and having achieved this in 1964, he moved on. He toured with his friend John Hanson, and spent two years working with Joan Littlewood in her company at the Theatre Royal, Stratford East.

In 1967 Jimmy created the TV series "Dad's Army" and, in association with David Croft, wrote eighty episodes. He received the Writers' Guild of Great Britain Award for the best TV comedy script in 1969, 1970 and 1971. He composed the signature tune "Who Do You Think You Are Kidding Mr. Hitler" for the series, and this was given the Ivor Novello Award for the best TV signature tune in 1970/71. He created the TV series "It Ain't Half Hot Mum" and, again with David Croft, wrote fifty-four episodes of this. He also composed the signature tune "Meet the Gang".

In addition, Jimmy Perry created and wrote "The Gnomes of Dulwich" for BBC TV and "Lollipop" for ATV. In 1981 he created the TV series "Hi De Hi", also writing its signature tune "Holiday Rock" and he worked on the BBC2 series "The Old Boy Network". "Hi De Hi" finished in 1987 after sixty episodes.

This year Jimmy is working on a fourth series of "You Rang M'Lord?", his new hit show with David Croft for BBC TV.

Jimmy also presents his own show on BBC TV, "Turns". This consists of rare clips of archival film of British Music Hall artistes.

Jimmy is the Curator of the world famous legendary "Grand Order of Water Rats" and it is at their museum in London that "Turns" is recorded.

In 1978 Jimmy Perry received the OBE in the Queen's Birthday Honours.

So many people who love the music hall talk about the great artists of the past, Marie Lloyd, Dan Leno, Joe Elvin and dozens of others. What were they really like? Were they as good as our grandparents kept telling us?

In 1901 Little Titch was filmed giving a performance in a Paris music hall (he was enormously popular in France). The film lasted only about 45 seconds, no music, no laughter and no audience reaction, the film was of course, silent. Little chance from this flickering shadow to see what this great artist was really like. Then with the invention of the sound film in 1928 everything changed. For the first time in history we could actually hear, as well as see, these great performers working.

My father, who died at the age of 92 many years ago, loved the music hall, or "Turns" as he used to call them, my mother never shared his enthusiasm, and so he frequently took me with him. We lived in South London in Barnes, a short bus ride from Hammersmith. It was the mid-1930's and what a different world it was, times were very hard, but we were amongst the fortunate few and comparatively well off.

I can remember sitting on the top of a number 9 bus with my father, and as we came over Hammersmith Bridge I could see the lights of Hammersmith Broadway in the distance. To this day I shall never forget how my heart pounded with excitement. There were three Variety Theatres to choose from, the Hammersmith Palace, Shepherds Bush Empire and the Chiswick Empire.

We sat in the third row of the stalls, a great privilege, boys of ten always wore short trousers in those days and the moquette on the seats used to chaff the back of my legs, but I didn't care, I was in paradise. I remember so well the smell of cigarette smoke (everyone smoked at that time) oranges and Jayes fluid. Then the conductor came into the orchestra pit, the lights went down and the overture struck up, and for the next two hours I was lost in a wonderful world.

Max Miller, Gracie Fields, Vic Oliver, Tessy O'Shea and Billy Bennett were just a few of the great variety stars that I was fortunate to see at the height of their fame. But I was also privileged to see some of the music hall veterans who were still going strong: Gus Elen, Harry Champion, George Robey and Kate Carney. And I can even remember seeing Sam Mayo, who sat at the piano wearing a shabby old dressing gown and a scratch wig, singing plaintive little songs like "Where do flies go in the winter time?" It was a magic world and I just couldn't wait to get up there on the stage and enter it. A world that for me, felt so safe. I shall always be thankful to my father for introducing me to something that has been a great love in my life ever since.

When I came home from the Far East after the war, I said to my parents, "I've made up my mind, I'm going into show busi-

ness" there was a long pause and my father said, "what a wonderful profession, I'm sure you'll do very well."

As Arthur Askey used to say "the page of history turns" and in 1978 I had a call from a BBC Producer, Don Sayer. He told me he had an idea to do a series on the life stories of some of the great variety comedians, he pointed out that as most of them were in their seventies and in some cases eighties, it was the last chance to preserve their work for people to remember. He asked me if I would like to help him put the shows together, I was delighted. And so we set about making the series "The Old Boy Network".

I never liked the title of the show, but the idea was wonderful. We did two series, the first featured Tommy Trinder, Arthur Askey, Sandy Powell, Jack Warner, Fred Emney and John Laurie. You might think that John

The inimitable Gracie Fields, a multi-talented variety artiste

Laurie was a strange choice amongst all those comedians, John was after all a distinguished actor and verse speaker, and I had quite a struggle to convince Don Sayer that he was a good choice. I had worked with John for nearly ten years on "Dad's Army" and, to me, he was one of the funniest men I ever met.

The format of the shows was very simple, we recorded them in various theatres before a live audience and each comedian told his life story, which was illustrated by film clips and photographs. I'd worked out the running order and crouched in the orchestra pit with large white cue cards so that the comedians didn't lose their place. The finished shows ran for forty minutes, but we usually recorded well over an hour's material.

Once they got the bit between their teeth and warmed to the audience there was no stopping them. They would go off at a tangent and put in material we hadn't rehearsed. I frantically pointed to the cue cards, but it was no use they simply ignored me and the audience loved it. In the end it didn't really matter. When we had edited the show down to the right length the result was magic.

As the life stories of these old comedians unfolded, they talked about other great artists they had worked with, and we needed film clips of them to illustrate the story; It was then that I made a wonderful discovery, the Pathe film library. From 1930 - 1960 a programme called Pathe Pictorial was shown in cinemas every week, it dealt with topical matters and information of the period, and lasted about 15 minutes, but the great thing was, it always finished with a variety turn. We spent weeks looking at all this material, with artists like Robb

Robb Wilton. Thanks to television, just as popular today, as he was 50 years ago.

Wilson, Gus Elen, Lily Morris and dozens of others. The thrill of watching these old variety performers come to life after so many years was a delight.

It was while we were looking at all this material, that the researcher on the programme, Jane Greenhill, suggested that I should present a programme of these clips, and this eventually led to the series "Turns". I have made three series in the past ten years, eighteen half hours of sheer delight.

The success of "Turns" has been amazing, and I have received thousands of letters, not only from older people, who remember seeing them in their youth, but from the younger generation, who were born long after these great variety turns were dead and gone.

Of all the film clips I showed on "Turns" perhaps the one that caused the greatest excitement was Wilson, Keppel and Betty, the eccentric dancers. Their act, "Cleopatra's Nightmare" was world famous and topped the bill everywhere in the 1930's and 1940's. Fortunately, there is quite a lot of them on film and I was able to include their act in each series.

Every time they were shown I got a huge amount of mail asking for more and they suddenly became famous again after an interval of 40 years. It is an amazing fact that, in one showing on television, more people saw Wilson, Keppel and Betty than all the theatre audiences during their entire career.

Robb Wilton was another turn that the viewers loved. This popular Liverpool comedian also caught the viewers' imagination, and I showed his famous sketches "The Police Station", "The Fire Station" and of course his great character Mr Muddlecombe JP in "The Magistrate". Thanks to television, Robb Wilton is just as popular today, as he was 50 years ago.

The first time I showed the comedienne Lily Morris doing her famous number "Why Am I Always the Bridesmaid?" the switchboard of the BBC was jammed with calls

Wilson, Keppel & Betty. More people saw them in one night on television than during their entire career on the halls.

27

Lily Morris. The switchboard at the BBC was jammed with calls from viewers.

Max was banned by the BBC in the 1930's. Lord Reith is reputed to have said, "I will not have that low comedian polluting the airways." Listening to recordings of Max Miller, his material seems very mild in comparison with today's humour.

With the arrival of commercial television, Max made several appearances, and we are lucky to have some old black and white video recordings of him working to an audience. Even though he was in his sixties, one can still see the old magic shining through. Sadly, it was only towards the end of his life that he was recognised as one the greatest stand-up comedians that this country has ever produced. I was also very lucky to discover film of some of the great veterans of the music hall that I mentioned earlier on.

In 1932 at the age of 70 the great cockney comedian Gus Elen went into the Pathe studios in Wardour Street and recorded several of his most popular songs, and it is thanks to these rare film clips that we can

from viewers demanding to have more of this wonderful lady in the series. They didn't really understand that I had recorded the programme many months before. They were so carried away by her performance that they didn't realise that Lily Morris had been dead for over 30 years.

The great Max Miller appeared in many feature films in the 1930's. His first screen appearance was in 1931 in J.B. Priestly's "Good Companions" with John Gielgud. Max had a small part as a music publisher and almost stole the picture. This led to a very successful career in British pictures including a series of films, "Educated Evans", in which he played a book maker and Albert Whelan played a police inspector, alas, all these films have been lost. In the film, "Hoots Mon" in which he starred with Florence Desmond, Max does his act, but it is a pale shadow of the real Max, who needed an audience to bounce off.

Max Miller, pictured with Henry Hall. Max was thought too rude for BBC TV

Gus Elen. The Victorian cockney dialect he used has now disappeared.

Unfortunately, all these clips were on nitrate film which disintegrates with the passing of time. I shall never forget coming across a tin with the words 'Billy Bennett' on it. We were all very excited at such a discovery, but when we opened it there was just a mass of jelly inside, the only record of a great music hall performer lost forever.

Fortunately, we have managed to save quite a few of these great musical artists by transferring them onto modern safety film, so in generations to come, for the first time in the history of mankind, people will be able to look at these wonderful "Silver Ghosts" and understand the pleasure they gave to audiences perhaps 200 years before.

Gracie Fields picture courtesy of the BBC Photo Library. Rest courtesy of Mander & Mitchenson.

see and hear a man who was born in Pimlico, London 130 years ago. The Victorian cockney dialect he uses has now disappeared, it is the same dialect that Charles Dickens used when he created Sam Weller.

Even more amazing to find film clips of Charles Coborn famous for "The Man who Broke the Bank at Monte Carlo" and "Two Lovely Black Eyes". He was born in 1852 and lived to be 93. When I first saw him on film I found it almost impossible to believe that I was watching a man who was born before the Crimean War.

Of course, one could only get a rough idea of these wonderful artists from the clips. They were filmed cold in a cramped basement studio in Wardour Street, they just stood in front of the camera and did their act. With no audience to react to. The big names got 12 guineas and the supporting acts 6.

Charles Coburn. Almost impossible to believe, I was watching a man born before the Crimean War.

TICKETS

L OCCASIONS
T-CONCERTS

CARMEN JONES
ME AND MY GIRL
OUR SONG
JOSEPH AND THE AMAZING
TECHNICOLOUR DREAMCOAT
SHADER
BLOOD BROTHERS

ERS

ows
Now

ALL SPORTING EVENTS INCLUDING
WIMBLEDON TENNIS
INTERNATIONAL RUGBY
FOOTBALL (CUP FINALS)
BOXING, GOLF ETC

2337

SS ROAD WC2

VARIETY ON STAGE
BY PETER HEPPLE
OF "THE STAGE & TELEVISION TODAY"

Although it is over 50 years ago since I saw my first Variety bill, I was too late to see some of the "greats" - Will Fyffe, Billy Bennett, Sir Harry Lauder. My generation grew up in the war years, and got a taste for Variety in its post-war boom period, little realising that only ten years later it would be on its way out.

From 1950 until the last of the great London suburban Variety theatres closed in 1960, I reported on it professionally, transferring then to covering the London and provincial cabaret clubs, which we thought in those days were Variety's logical successors, as many of the acts had gone into them. Alas, these were comparatively short-lived, though they died more because of the breathalyser and the gaming regulations than through any fault of their own.

The very first Variety bill I can remember seeing was sometime in the 1930s at Finsbury Park Empire, topped by Jack Hylton and his Band, though my recollections are less of the music, despite the presence as a guest with the band of the great tenor sax stylist Coleman Hawkins, than the comedy antics of one of Hylton's sax section, Freddy Schweitzer, who I thought was one of the funniest men I had ever seen.

But the fact that a dance band topped the bill was the reason why I had persuaded my father to take me for dance bands were one of the most popular features on radio in the thirties and I was one of their keenest fans, even though I was only nine years old. I was not alone, because as soon as the BBC had begun transmitting regular dance band broadcasts in the early thirties, followed by the formation of its own BBC Dance Orchestra, led first by Jack Payne and then by Henry Hall, theatre owners realised they were on to a good thing.

Just about every broadcasting band - Ambrose, Roy Fox, Jack Payne, Harry Roy, Billy Cotton, to name just a few - went out on Variety tours, deserting the West End nightspots to do so, and I don't suppose I was the only one to develop a taste for the rest of the Variety bill, the comedians, the dancers, the speciality acts, through going to see the bands we had heard on the radio.

The bands, moreover, were usually a show in themselves, for leaders realised that when they went on stage they had to entertain, putting in plenty of comedy numbers, showcasing their singers and bringing out the hitherto hidden talents of their musicians, some of whom became standard Variety acts in their own right - singers like Elsie Carlisle, Sam Browne and Evelyn Dall, musicians like Max Bacon, Nat Gonella and George Elrick.

In the thirties, and indeed right up to the fifties, radio was the great promotional medium. A successful appearance on the BBC's Saturday Night Music Hall before the war could lead to a full date-book for Variety acts which had been toiling around the country without much reward.

The immediate post-war Variety Bandbox brought to the fore a host of young artists who had developed while in the forces, among them Peter Sellers, Frankie Howerd, Max Bygraves and Tony Hancock. A remarkable post-war example of sudden radio renown was Donald Peers, who had been in the business for nearly 20 years but shot to superstardom in 1949 when he was given a radio series.

Howard Keel, one of many Americans to play the London Palladium.

By the fifties, when the first record charts were brought into being, radio was superseded by records as a route to instant stardom, and it might be said that the life of Variety was extended by this means.

Many American performers who had a Number One hit, like Guy Mitchell and the almost-forgotten Charlie Gracie and Mitchell Torok, not to mention the first country singer to make an impression on British audiences, Slim Whitman, played both West End theatres like the London Palladium and the leading provincial houses.

We also produced some recording stars of our own - Alma Cogan, Petula Clark, Lee Lawrence, Ronnie Hilton, Robert Earl, all of whom toured in Variety. It should not be forgotten that both Tommy Steele and Cliff Richard looked to Variety to capitalise on their recording fame, appearing on the Moss and Stoll circuits with a supporting bill of comedians, acrobats and jugglers.

The Variety format was more or less retained for the first package shows, usually of one-nighters, put out by Larry Parnes and other promoters. The main attractions may have been four or five recording artists, but there was at least one lesser-known act of solid professional value and a comedy compere such as Jimmy - then known as Jim - Tarbuck.

Though many of these teenage stars have dropped out of sight, it is worth noting that some survivors, for instance Lonnie Donegan and Joe Brown, would be still at home in Variety.

What, young people sometimes ask me, was Variety really like, perhaps conscious of the fact that when they attend a live

Jimmy Tarbuck provided an important role as comedy compere of variety shows.

Although the practice declined towards the end of the Variety era, the number of each item on the programme was indicated on an illuminated panel on the side of the proscenium arch, useful in case there was a change in the running order.

Two features about Variety always remain in my mind. The first is that it is classless and ageless. Devised by such pioneers as Sir Oswald Stoll as a family entertainment, audiences ranged from children to grand-parents and many families occupied the same seats on the same night each week. Monday nights, traditionally the worst of the week, was when the agents came in and most of the "comps", distributed to those tradespeople who displayed bills, were used.

The second was that there was always something interesting, even if some shows were invariably better than others. An artist like Max Miller - who incidentally never did more than about 35 minutes on stage - had his regular following, of course, and could play all the leading London theatres at least once and sometimes twice a year, confining his other dates to halls in Southern England.

But many bills did not rely on one star artist. Variety was, after all, the name of the game and it was quite likely that a show with eight or nine acts would have four and sometimes five tops of the bill, the Number One spot going to the artist whose name was on the left-hand side. This was often as true of the Palladium as East Ham Palace.

If there was sometimes disappointment at the performance of the top of the bill there were invariably compensations in the rest of the show, and looking back now I realise that Variety brought me into contact, in its

concert at a vast and often uncomfortable venue in which one group or artist may hold the stage for two hours or more they may be subjecting themselves to an experi-ence rather than entertainment.

Well, it was invariably twice-nightly, at times like 6.15 and 8.45, the shows gener-ally lasted two hours and there was a ten-minute interval in which it was practically impossible to get a drink, mainly because the bar was small and drinking was not regarded as a necessary part of the enter-tainment. If you wanted a drink before or after the show there was usually a pub next door. There was a pit orchestra, often of not a particularly high standard, in which the conductor and drummer were the key members, and even recording stars were expected to content themselves with this accompaniment, though they usually brought their own pianists.

THE LONDON
COLISEUM
CHARING CROSS.

Managing Director — Sir OSWALD STOLL
Manager — ARTHUR CROXTON

Monday, April 9, 1923
TWICE DAILY at 2-30 and 7-45
CHANGE OF PROGRAMME WEEKLY!

GEORGE GROSSMITH & J. A. E. MALONE
PRESENT
GEORGE GROSSMITH'S
PRODUCTION OF
THE
OFFENBACH FOLLIES
Music Arranged by JOHN ANSELL. Lyrics by ADRIAN ROSS
FEATURING
NANCY LOVAT
GWENDOLEN BROGDEN
GEORGE BISHOP
LYELL JOHNSTON
AND 22 OTHER ARTISTES

ONE WEEK ONLY
CARL HYSON
PEG HARRIS
AND JACK HOWARD
WITH HIS "MIDNIGHT FOLLIES" BAND
FROM THE METROPOLE, LONDON.

MISS GRACE — LAST WEEK
CRISTIE
OF "MASKS AND BUBBLES" FAME.
LYRIC-DANCING SUPREME.
THE OUTSTANDING SENSATION OF
"THE LEAGUE OF NOTIONS."

MOVING EVENTS ON THE SCREEN

HILDA — ONE WEEK ONLY
NELSON
Presents "GEMS OF MELODY." Featuring
PATRICIA ROSSBOROUGH Pianist; PETER BUSCANY Cellist

AMAC
Assisted by MLLE. VELMA.
PRESENTS HIS NOVEL
THREE CARD ILLUSION — ONE WEEK ONLY

THE SCOTTISH NATIONAL THEATRE SOCIETY present — LAST WEEK
THE
SCOTTISH NATIONAL PLAYERS
(Under the Direction of ANDREW P. WILSON).
IN A COMEDY IN ONE ACT,
"A VALUABLE RIVAL" By NEIL F. GRANT

A. E. ANDERSSON presents — LAST WEEK
THE FAMOUS
SWEDISH HAND-BELL RINGERS

THE
DORMONDES
Presenting "SCIENTIFIC NONSENSE."

FRANK — ONE WEEK ONLY
PICHEL AND SCALE
NOVELTY COMEDY ACROBATS

PRICES AS USUAL. Telephone Booking Office 7540 Gerrard (5 lines)
CHILDREN UNDER TWELVE HALF-PRICE TO ALL PARTS AT AFTERNOON PERFORMANCES, EXCEPT BANK HOLIDAYS. Children in arms not admitted.

own modest way, with the other arts. It was not the World Cup that introduced me to "Nessun Dorma" but a singer in Variety over 40 years ago, and that was because Jussi Bjorling made a record which was often played on Forces Favourites.

I suppose that the elegant and graceful act of the Ganjou Brothers and Juanita, or perhaps their compatriots Halama and Konarski, made me aware of the joys of dance. Certainly my appreciation of jazz was stimulated by the Quintette du Hot

Club de France, with Django Reinhardt and Stephane Grappelli, who toured Variety theatres, and our own Joe Daniels and his Hot Shots, undoubtedly a show band but which was based on "hot music".

And then there were the young comedians, who generally had to start "down the bill". I remember seeing Dickie Henderson as a 14-year-old at Newcastle Empire in 1938, though he was a tap dancer in those days, Morecambe and Wise and Des O'Connor buried among the "wines and spirits" at Finsbury Park, Frankie Howerd nervously topping the cast of a touring revue, in which the male singer was John Watts; later John Hanson, Bill Maynard, Max Bygraves, Ron Moody, Tony Hancock and Bob Monkhouse long before they became household names.

A Variety bill during the fifties invariably began with a dancing act, among my favourites being McAndrews and Mills - Keith McAndrews now looks after the affairs of Ken Dodd - and Morgan and Grey - Rex Grey, who died last year, became one of our best floorshow producers. The dancers also opened the second half and the closing spot was filled, not by the top of the bill, but often by an eye-catching speciality act, strong enough to keep the audience in their seats, so that there was no rush for the exit once the star had finished.

Second spot was usually by a young comedian, there was sometimes a musical speciality - who better than the Musical Elliotts? - and in those days we had enough home-produced speciality acts to fill the rest of the bill. One or two, like the never-forgotten Wilson, Keppel and Betty, and the Two Pirates, were big enough names to warrant special billing.

The diet of Variety was varied by pantomime, naturally, but also by revue which was a genre which got a bad name because they invariably had titles like Bad Girls from Paris and Nudes of the World and featured nude posing acts and rather genteel strippers, though few performed with the delicacy and taste of Phyllis Dixey, the West End wartime favourite who later went out on tour, and Christabel Leighton-Porter, better known as Jane of the Daily Mirror.

But before nudity gained the upper hand, revue had a good reputation, though it figured more often in the programmes at the No.2 and No.3 theatres than in the major houses. The No.1s often had touring versions of West End revue successes, such as Piccadilly Hayride, with the same scenery and costumes but lesser names in the cast. Even Bernard Delfont's Folies Bergere show, which had a long run in the West End, toured with all its elaborate scenic effects.

For the smaller theatres, however, revue was often a better proposition than Variety. For one thing, all the bigger box office attractions were obviously tied up with the Moss and Stoll circuits, summer shows and major pantomimes.

Revue offered anything up to eight dancers, a principal comedian and his straight man - the latter being almost invariably the company manager - a musical speciality act, one of whose members was probably the musical director, a soubrette and probably one or two utility artists who could dance and put across a song and were invaluable in the comedy sketches.

In the fifties, most of them had a "naughty" title which often promised more than it

36

Founded
SEPTEMBER 1963

"Cherishing the jewels of the past and actively supporting the interests of the future"

Live Shows: 1st Tuesday of each month.
Full details from:
Membership Secretary: Wendy Lunn,
74 Turnpike Drive, Luton, Beds LU3 3RF

delivered, but there were variations on the theme. For some years after the war there was a spate of all-male revues, in which the artists were alleged to have entertained the forces. They had such titles as "Soldiers in Skirts", "We Were in the Forces" and, most notably, "Forces Showboat", which starred a very fine double act called Bartlett and Ross, superb Ugly Sisters in pantomime, as were the "Soldiers in Skirts" stars, Ford and Sheen.

For some time "Forces Showboat" also featured Harry Secombe, doing the shaving routine with which he first rose to stage fame, and in the chorus was Danny La Rue, then using his real name of Danny Carroll.

Revue performers were something of a special breed, who seldom aspired to the No.1s, though I remember Arthur Haynes as a principal comedian in one at the Queen's, Poplar, and Bernie Winters was in another as one of the utility people, with a five-minute spot of his own near the beginning of the show.

Yet I for one have happy memories of the skill and good humour of such touring revue comedians as Curly Jay, Harry Rowson and Phil Strickland, all of whom are forgotten, and one or two who did achieve later fame on television, like Ted Lune and Jack Haig.

Being a Variety goer for over twenty years I look back fondly on the early years, occasionally wondering whether it will ever have a major revival, taking it back to its heyday. Probably not yet, for we are now in the era of "niche marketing", in which even entertainment is sold to specialist groups, with what is left of Variety, as I remember it, being consigned to the "nostalgia" category.

But in its haphazard, enjoyably eclectic way, Variety widened my horizons and we were seldom bored by it. For it was expected that first and foremost artists should entertain during the relatively short time they were on stage, and it even rubbed off on the apprentice rock and rollers of the early sixties. Could this be why Tommy Steele, Cliff Richard, Gerry and the Pacemakers, Joe Brown and Freddie and the Dreamers are still in the business over 30 years since they began?

Coliseum bill courtesy of Roy Hudd. All other pictures courtesy of Alan Whitehead of the London Palladium.

Tommy Steele learnt the art of performance on variety bills.

VARIETY ON RADIO
A PERSONAL MEMORY
BY MIKE CRAIG

In the last twenty eight years, Mike Craig has been responsible for writing or producing over one thousand comedy shows for Television and Radio. In the sixties and seventies he wrote for Harry Worth, Ken Dodd, Hinge and Bracket, Roy Castle, Des O'Connor, "Selwyn Froggit", Jimmy Tarbuck and Morecambe and Wise, including the classic 1976 Eric and Ernie Christmas Show, when Angela Rippon bared her legs.

In 1977 Mike became a BBC Radio Light Entertainment Producer, and has a string of successes to his credit, in particular his award winning Grumbleweed's Radio Series, the memorable Al Read Shows - "Such is Life", the popular Jimmy Cricket Show - "Jimmy's Cricket Team" and his own long running interview programme - "It's a Funny Business".

Over the last ten years he has proved to be one of P & O's most popular lecturers, entertaining thousands of 'Canberra' and 'Sea Princess' passengers with his series of one man shows - "Mike Craig's ABC of Comedy".

Mike is one of the most sought after 'After Dinner Speakers' in the country, a Lord's Taverner, and Scribe Rat of the 'Grand Order of Water Rats'. In March 1988 he was given a Tribute Lunch by the Variety Club of Great Britain to mark his twenty five year contribution to comedy.

Hands up all those who remember Eric Maschwitz, Stanford Robinson, Harry S. Pepper and John Sharman. No? Alright then, how about Charlie Shadwell, Ernest Longstaffe and John Watt. No good?

Well let's try some programmes. 'Songs from the Shows', 'Garrison Theatre', 'The Old Town Hall', 'Monday Night at Eight' and 'In Town Tonight'.

Still no good? Well then you'd better pack in and read something else because if you never curled up on the dining room carpet (or even the front room carpet if your parents owned an 'Extension Speaker') and listened, with your head close to your wireless, to Eric Coates' 'Knightsbridge March' herald another 'In Town Tonight', then you've missed out on a memorable piece of radio magic. "Violets, lovely violets.

Get your violets," came the weekly cry from Mrs. Baker battling vocally in the middle of Piccadilly Circus against the 'mighty roar of London's traffic', which was stopped, on cue at 7.30 every Saturday Night.

How did they do it? The traffic actually stopped!! I heard it. How I wanted to see it happen. Ah, the joy of the wireless. I never realised until I checked on the programme's enormous run, but 'In Town Tonight' was the first twenty five years of my life! Lionel Gamlin, Michael Standing, John Ellison and of course Brian Johnston were my 'friends'. The format has never been bettered. A format heard by the listener for the first time on November 10th 1933. That was a very significant year for Radio Variety. The year, in fact, that the BBC Variety Department 'separated' from Val Gielgud's 'Drama' umbrella. In charge of this new baby was Eric Maschwitz (you <u>must</u> remember his lyrics for - 'These Foolish Things' and 'A Nightingale Sang in Berkley Square'. You do? Then welcome back!).

It is totally impossible in an article of this length to pay tribute to the tremendous contribution made by the aforementioned (and many more) Producers, Musical Directors and Programmes in that pioneering era. An era which was to bring laughter, good clean family laughter, into millions of homes; but more importantly an era which slowly but surely, under the guiding hand of Eric Maschwitz, created the foundations for an Entertainment Department second to none. An Entertainment Department which would grow steadily over the years bringing millions of hours of quality music and comedy into our own homes.

The first attempt to bring 'Variety' as we know it into our homes was to simply broadcast, LIVE, a section of a Variety Bill from a provincial theatre. As early as 1926 the BBC had relayed a section of the Royal Variety Performance, live, from the

Arthur Askey at the microphone.

Alhambra, London; but now theatres from Halifax to Sunderland, from New Cross to the beautiful jewel, the Argyle, Birkenhead, got their chance to be 'on the Air'. Who were on those Bills I wonder? I guarantee there were one or two destined to become household names via this wonderful medium.

Radio's 'Household Names' are endless. Sandy Powell, Tommy Handley, Arthur Askey, Kenneth Horne, Richard Murdoch, Gert and Daisy, Vera Lynn, The Western Brothers, Donald Peers, Michael Howard, Frankie Howerd, Derek Roy, Jimmy Edwards and Co, Jimmy Clitheroe, Charlie Chester, Peter Cavanagh, Bob and Alf Pearson, Al Read, those idiots 'larking' in the Navy, 'Big Bill Campbell and his Rocky Mountain Rhythm', Hancock, Ken Dodd, Secombe, Sellers and Milligan.

And then there were the shows. 'Happidrome', 'Mr Muddlecombe, J.P.', 'Ignorance is Bliss', 'I.T.M.A.', 'Variety Bandbox', 'Variety Fanfare', 'Palace of Varieties', 'Blackpool Night', 'Workers'

Mike interviewed Elsie Waters shortly before her death. She was 'Gert' of Gert and Daisy.

Playtime', 'Much Binding', 'The Billy Cotton Band Show', 'Hoop-La', 'Up the Pole', 'Our Shed', 'Educating Archie', 'Ray's a Laugh', 'Hi Gang', 'Beyond our Ken', 'Life with the Lyons', 'The Clitheroe Kid', 'Round the Horne', 'Waterlogged Spa' and 'Stand Easy'.

What an incredible range! All memorable, and most of them timeless. You don't believe me? Well if you doubt the power of the Wireless, the lasting quality of the 'comedy word' then complete the following rhyme in no more than six words (answers on a postcard please)

Down in the jungle,
living in a tent ...

See what I mean? It's easy isn't it? Now try this one. Complete the second line.

We three, in Happidrome.
Working for the BBC ...

It's amazing isn't it? The first time you heard those lines broadcast on Radio was nearly fifty years ago; and doesn't it give you pleasure to be able to remember them? Just think what we would have missed without those firm foundations laid by Maschwitz and built on by a succession of producers who cared. From it emerged the present BBC Light Entertainment Department. What a debt laughter lovers owe Maschwitz and his successors. I don't know of any other Broadcasting Organisation in the world that has a Department solely dedicated to the discovering, encouraging and presenting of comedy performer and writer.

Radio memories are forever. Ask anybody you like over forty, Sunday lunchtime WAS Al Read. It WAS Billy Cotton. (Fancy being told to 'Wakey Wakey' when you're half way through your roast beef and yorkshire pudding!). It was glorious, uplifting stuff. And without this great department, would the Nation, during the War and after, have put a smile on each other's faces with the lines ... 'I don't mind if I do?' ... 'Mighty Fine!' ... 'I go, I come back' ... 'I've arrived and to prove it I'm here' ... 'A good idea, son!'? We all said them. They became part

Recording the many memories of Al Read for Mike's series - "Such is Life".

THE ARCADIAN FOLLIES
will amuse listeners tonight at 9.0 with a Variety entertainment
relayed from the South Pier, Blackpool

A topical s...

'Surprise items'
arranged after t...
been very popul...
feature is desig...
minute items
programmes.
entertainment,
the...

Northern Variety

There will be a relay tonight
from the stage of the
ARGYLE THEATRE, BIRKENHEAD,
at 7.10

8.0 'MUSIC...
HERMION...
(The cele...
C...

9.0 VARIETY BANDBOX
from the
Kilburn Empire, London with Albert Modley
The Radio Revellers, Beryl Orde
Tollefsen, Robert Moreton, Stella Nicols,
Gate Eastly, Jackie Allen and Barbara
Billy Ternent and his Orchestra
Introduced by Philip Slessor
Produced by Bryan Sears
Repeat Saturday at 1.10 (Home)

of our vocabulary. My father at the age of 84 was still saying 'After you Claude' when we left a room together. I dutifully replied - 'No, after you Cecil'.

Yes, the catch phrase. Until funny men went on the wireless there had never been a vehicle for someone to say 'Can you hear me mother?' and instantaneously half the Nation hear it. Likewise the 'Signature Tune'. That wonderful aperitif which captured the flavour and put you in the mood for what was to follow. It became obligatory for every artiste *and* every programme to have its own signature tune. It's impossible to list them, there were hundreds.

'Hello again, we're on the radi-o again' sang Geraldo's boys, 'Ring that bell, bang that drum' screamed Charlie Chester and his mob, 'Such is Life, Life is what you make it' wrote Ronnie Taylor for Al Read, and what must be - in my opinion - the most original

BBC radio's Henry Hall's Guest Night. This '50s line-up shows, l to r: David Hughes, Al Fernhead, Stan Emeney, Freddie Holmes, Art Reed, Paul Fenhoulet, Henry Hall, Alastair Scott-Johnston, Beryl Reid, Max Miller, Robin Richmond & Dickie Henderson.

and cleverly thought out signature tune of them all ... 'At Much Binding in the Marsh, (Tiddle-um Pom Pom)'. I couldn't have imagined life without Murdoch and Horne's weekly input into those so clever verses.

I must mention the organ and the dance bands, (my father would never forgive me if I didn't). Remember the three Reginalds? (Foort, Porter-Browne and Dixon) and Sandy Macpherson with his 'Chapel in the Valley'? I wonder, would the organ have emerged as a home instrument without its introduction into the home by radio? I've mentioned Geraldo, but what about the other dance bands? Henry Hall with his two signature tunes and his immortal catch phrase. 'Good evening, everyone. This is Henry Hall speaking, and tonight is my Guest Night!' How I loved it when Betty Driver sang 'The Sailor with the Navy Blue

Eyes'. Betty lives round the corner from me now, I never ever go and see her without bringing up the subject of Henry Hall. That's what radio does to you. As I said before - Radio memories are for ever.

Then there was the elegance and sophistication of Ambrose and his vocalist Les Allen late on a Saturday night. Maurice Winnick whose signature tune told you he played 'The Sweetest Music This Side of Heaven', Jack Payne, who 'Said it with Music', Carroll Gibbons, always 'On the Air', Billy Ternent, who stooged for everybody on 'Variety Bandbox', Nat Temple, who breakfasted with Braden, and the inimitable Harry Roy who was everybody's favourite.

Yes, the BBC Variety Department touched us all. My own childhood favourite was 'Music Hall', produced by John Sharman. (I share a great honour with this man. We are the only BBC Radio producers ever to be admitted into the Grand Order of Water Rats). Eight o'clock every Saturday during the war I was there. The voice of Norman Wooland opening the show, declaiming like a Shakespearian actor ... "Good evening ladies and gentlemen - MUSIC HALL," Charles Shadwell and the BBC Variety Orchestra crashing in with the signature tune - 'The Spice of Life', cue applause, and the shivers went down my back. Norman Wooland.

I loved him, loved his voice, yet had no idea who he was. Then one day in 1956 I saw Lawrence Olivier's film 'Richard the Third' and suddenly heard one of the actors talking like Norman Wooland. It was all there. "My Leige, my noble Leige. I bring thee ... MUSIC HALL!!" The credits confirmed it. It <u>was</u> Norman Wooland. <u>My</u> Norman Wooland! He <u>was</u> a Shakespearian actor!! I was slightly annoyed. Can you imagine the disappointment? I thought he introduced 'Music Hall' for a living.

To me 'Music Hall' captured all the atmosphere and excitement of the greatest love of my life - The Variety Theatre. You see I'd seen them all at the Dewsbury Empire from the age of six. Suzette Tarri, Albert Modley, Cavan O'Connor, Harry Lester and his Hayseeds, Stainless Stephen, Nosmo King, Jimmy James, Mario (Harp) Lorenzi, The Radio Revellers, Beryl Orde, Morton Fraser's Harmonica Gang, Morris and Cowley, Rob Wilton, - and now I could <u>hear</u> them on <u>my</u> 'Music Hall'. It <u>was</u> mine you see, because it came out of my loud speaker. That was and still is the beauty of radio. It's yours. You can listen on your own and hear performer <u>AND</u> audience. You're privileged. You are sitting in the grandest box of all, suspended above

performer and audience. Long may it continue. Thank you Eric Maschwitz for building the greatest Variety Empire of them all.

Oh, before I sign off, I can't leave that enormous traffic jam in Piccadilly Circus or else nobody will be able to get to the BBC Paris Studio for this week's recording of 'News Huddlines!' Just put your fingers in your ears for a minute, I'm going to shout. "Carry on, London!"

Colour Photographs courtesy of Mike Craig; Radio Times data courtesy of Mike Craig & the BBC; black & white photographs courtesy of BBC Photo Library.

'MUSIC-HALL'

HERMIONE BADDELEY
(The celebrated Stage Star)

CHARLES AUSTIN and CO.

ETHEL LEVEY
(The famous Revue Artist)

NORMAN LONG
(A Song, a Joke and a Piano)

DERICKSON and BROWN
DUNCAN GRAY
(Just a Comedian)

THE EIGHT STEP SISTERS
(Trained by Mrs RODNEY HUDSON)

THE B.B.C. THEATRE ORCHESTRA
(Under the direction of S. KNEALE KELLEY)

A topical supplement - this evening at 7.30

'Surprise items', short broadcasts of topical interest arranged after the main programmes of the day, have been very popular in the past. This new Saturday night feature is designed to collect a number of these last minute items in a topical supplement to the week's programmes. It will consist of thirty minutes' diversified entertainment, varying in character every week with the personalities who happen to be 'in town tonight'.

THE BBC AND VARIETY
A PERSONAL MEMOIR
BY YVONNE LITTLEWOOD

Yvonne Littlewood recently retired from the BBC after over 40 years of service within BBC TV's Light Entertainment department. Her knowledge, stretching from broadcasts out of Alexandra Palace to the present TV Centre's output, encompasses all aspects of production and direction. From 1960 onwards, she produced and directed over 600 diverse shows for the Variety Department. In 1986 Ms Littlewood was awarded a much deserved MBE, for her services to broadcasting.

In the early days Variety on television derived its format from the tradition of the music hall - too early to develop a style of its own, programmes followed the pattern of the Variety bill - the speciality act, stand-up comedian, conjuror, singer, adagio act, and top of the bill, usually a leading comic or personality entertainer.

In the '30s many Variety artistes like Gracie Fields, George Robey, Stanley Holloway and Arthur Askey had contributed to experimental programmes for the new invention being pioneered by John Logie Baird.

When the BBC finally launched an official service on the 2nd November 1936 with both the Baird and Marconi-EMI systems the very first programme featured Adele Dixon, Buck and Bubbles (a coloured duo "versatile comedians who dance, play the piano, sing and cross chat") and the Lai Founs (oriental jugglers, four men and two women, who specialised in plate spinning).

The week continued with "Starlight" featuring Bebe Daniels and Ben Lyon, and the BBC Dance Orchestra directed by Henry Hall (whose soloists included Molly, Marie and Mary, Dan Donon and George Elrick). Although all programmes were only on the air for two hours a day - 3.00-4.00 and 9.00-10.00 pm - much of the time was devoted to Variety talent, often in only 10 or 15 minute items, but within a very few weeks Variety held a regular 35 minutes on Saturday night which was to remain a pattern for many years to come.

Other artistes who appeared in those early months included Ronald Frankau, Claude Dampier, Googie Withers (in song and dance!), Boyer and Ravel, the two Leslies (Sarony and Holmes), Robb Wilton, Gillie Potter (subtitled 'Auspicum Melioris aevi'), Sophie Tucker, Carroll Levis and his Discoveries, Hutch (Leslie A. Hutchinson), Tommy Handley, Flotsam and Jetsam, Cyril Fletcher, Hildegarde, Leslie Henson, Fred Emney, Richard Hearne, Yvonne Arnaud, Frances Day, Hermione Baddeley, Cyril Ritchard and Rawicz and Landauer.

All the major show bands of the day like Jack Payne, Jack Hylton and Geraldo joined Henry Hall, and most variety revue shows were accompanied by the Television Orchestra conducted by Hyam Greenbaum (known affectionately as Bumps!), husband of Sidonie Goosens who also regularly featured with her harp recitals. In one such programme she shared the billing with Margot Fonteyn (simply referred to in the billing as 'Dancer').

Cyril Fletcher, TV and Radio personality, reads his "Odour of the Week" on That's Life, 1974.

There were series "Burnt Sepia" and "Ebony" devoted to coloured artistes popular at the time, like Nina Mae McKinney, and a taste of what was happening in the West End featured excerpts from stage shows such as "On Your Toes", with the legendary Vera Zorina - who subsequently was also given her own 10 minute show!

In September 1939 television was closed down for the duration of the war and it was not until the 7th June 1946 that it started transmitting again. The show that re-opened the service was called "Variety Party" and included Mantovani and his Orchestra, Kay Cavendish, Peter Waring (in comedy), Beryl Orde (impressions), Jackie Hunter (Canadian comedian), Gwen Catley and The Three Admirals. That same evening there was music with Geraldo and his singers Carole Carr, Sally Douglas, Archie Lewis and Dick James. The following day the viewers saw the Beverly Sisters, and for twenty minutes to close the evening's programmes - Koringa and her Crocodiles!

Of course in the first years, both pre and post war, television was seen by comparatively few viewers and only in the London area (it was not until 1949 that it was accessible to the Midlands and early in the '50s before it reached further North and to Scotland, Wales and the West Country).

Whilst many variety artistes were interested in this new medium, as it reached an additional audience to that which frequented the theatres and music halls, when

Michael Bentine's Potty Time for BBC TV in the early '70s. Big Louie looks like he's put the frighteners on Michael.

The Late Joyce Grenfell pictured for her TV series in the '60s. The mistress of the monologue and funny song was a great TV favourite.

the number of viewers started to grow they accepted a contract with caution because many had more or less just one act (which they had lived off for years on the halls) - one exposure was to 'blow' the whole routine forever.

It is true to say that Wilson, Keppel and Betty refused to appear on television for this very reason. It is also reported that some agents threatened to black-list their clients who agreed to appear on the small screen.

But many famous names were to be found testing out the water in those first days after the war - Harry Secombe, Michael Bentine, Max Bygraves, Hattie Jacques, Jimmy Edwards, Vera Lynn, Richard Tauber, Jack Buchanan, Yves Montand, Julie

Andrews, Joseph Locke, Stephane Grappelli, Petula Clark, (like Julie Andrews, a very young singer), Joyce Grenfell, Adelaide Hall, Edmundo Ros ...

Series titles that will probably still be remembered by viewers who were around at the time included "Stars in Your Eyes", "Rooftop Rendezvous", "Saturday Night at the Palace", "Paging You", "Wit and Wisdom" with Norman Wisdom, "Regency Room" (with Ian Carmichael among its regular cast), and "The Passing Show" which told the story in words and music of the variety and musical theatre from 1900 to 1950.

An amazing amount was achieved out of the two not very large studios at Alexandra Palace. Often shows were rehearsed between 10.30 and 1.00 pm and then transmitted that same afternoon from 3 o'clock. On many occasions they were repeated the same evening or three or four days later! Everything had to be rehearsed

Pictured during "For Your Pleasure" for the BBC, Norman Wisdom sings "All The Things You Are."

Max Wall plays Professor Walloffski during the BBC show "Meet Max Wall" in the '50s.

and performed again because in those days there was no such thing as recording a show for repeat transmission.

There was always an interest in reflecting the European entertainment scene and in 1948 a lavish production was imported to Alexandra Palace when the entire Lido company was flown in from Paris just for one night - Bluebell Girls and all. Additional sections of costume were provided to ensure the famous Lido 'models' conformed to standards of decency for the television audience. The French management agreed to close their famous venue for one day but it turned into two when their return was delayed by fog at London Airport!

A home-produced and very popular French Cabaret style series was "Cafe Continental" introduced originally by Al Burnett but

probably better recalled with Helene Cordet as its hostess - it introduced a wide variety of continental acts. The orchestra for many variety shows and series at this time

Harry Worth in "Border Country", transmitted by the BBC in the late '60s.

was in the versatile hands of Eric Robinson who was later to have his own very successful showcase "Music for You".

The late '40s and early '50s saw the start of series headlined by a single star name - Terry Thomas in "How Do You View?", Charlie Chester, Vic Oliver, Frankie Howerd, Ted Ray, Eric Barker (& Pearl Hackney), and Arthur Askey in "Before Your Very Eyes"

Michael Bentine on "Goonreel" in the '50s. The programme was never quite the success on TV that it was on radio.

(with the statuesque Sabrina). A little later in the decade Tommy Trinder, Max Wall, Fred Emney, Charlie Drake and Harry Worth, Norman Evans, Bill Maynard, Terry Scott and Hugh Lloyd joined the roll of screen favourites in titles like "Tommy's Trinder Box", "Emney Enterprises", "Great Scott it's Maynard", "Hugh and I".

Jewel and Warriss (the first of many successful television double-acts) had a series "Turn it Up". This had to be mounted in the Bedford Theatre, Camden Town, in order to get the advantage of 'live' audience reaction. In 1953, by the time they appeared in a sequel "Re-Turn It Up", the BBC had bought the old Shepherds Bush Empire so it had its own theatre converted with full technical facilities, but retaining the old theatre seating and acoustics for artistes who needed to work in as near as possible a real music hall environment.

By the early '50s the BBC had also acquired the studios at Lime Grove so producers were at least given more space and facilities to expand their production ideas.

Special Variety shows always marked the opening of a new studio and in Coronation year a big gala "For Your Pleasure" was mounted on the occasion of the first visit to Lime Grove of Her Majesty the Queen and His Royal Highness the Duke of Edinburgh.

In regular schedules the ladies had a showcase in "Quite Contrary" introduced by Catherine Boyle. Ballroom dancing, always popular on the small screen, as "Come Dancing" has proved, took the floor at this time with Television Dancing Club - Victor Silvester giving weekly lessons on everything from the quickstep to the cha cha cha.

Producers looking out for new talent kept their eye on who was appearing at the Windmill Theatre (there were many young comedians who were pleased to get a chance to try out their new acts) and the Nuffield centre too. Of new recruits to television who had immediate success Dave King was one and, of course, Benny Hill who, with his own brand of inventive com-

A complete service for business:

edy over the next forty years, became probably the most internationally successful television comedy star ever.

At this time too, Michael Bentine was developing his own zany style of humour with "It's a Square World". The Goons even had a trial show on television "Goonreel" but it was in no way as successful as their show on radio, probably due to the fact that in the very early days the 'visualisation' of comedy of this kind was so much more difficult to achieve without the aid of today's sophisticated techniques.

But television did develop its own successful presentation of radio favourites and The Billy Cotton Band Show, with Russ Conway, Kathie Kay, Bill's team of singers and dancers and special guests (Max Bygraves, Alma Cogan, Roy Castle among the regulars) ran for many years. "Life with the Lyons" was another radio transfer to TV with Bebe Daniels and Ben Lyon and their children Richard and Barbara, also "Ask Pickles" Wilfred Pickles' successful roadshow.

With the new skiffle and rock crazes sweeping the country popular music had an ever increasing place in programme schedules - "Hit Parade" was a regular feature from the early '50s followed by the "Tin Pan Alley Show". The first record series was

Eric Morecombe delivers his trademark cheek tap to partner Ernie Wise!

"Off The Record" which started in 1955, introduced by Jack Payne. Later the presentation of pop music took a very different look with "Oh Boy", "Wham" and "Drumbeat", then followed "Six Five Special" introduced by Josephine Douglas and Pete Murray. "Top of the Pops" was a sequel to all those early pop shows and is now in its 28th year.

Panel and quiz shows were also getting big audiences to mention just "What's My Line?", "Find the Link", "Juke Box Jury" and "Ask Me Another". "This Is Your Life" had its regular spot on Monday evenings. In the late '50s and early '60s the era of the 'variety' show as we had known it definitely waned just as the days of traditional variety paled in the halls too.

Unique 'one off' performers like Ken Dodd, Spike Milligan, Tommy Cooper, Stanley Baxter, Marty Feldman and Joyce Grenfell had their own successful series but television had to find its own new talent and programmes were created to discover more potential stars of tomorrow. The BBC had a series called 'Camera One' and, of course, one of the longest running talent shows was ITV's 'Opportunity Knocks' hosted by Hughie Green - discovery time for Les Dawson, Russ Abbot, Cannon and Ball, Lena Zavaroni, Little and Large, and Freddie Starr. The Series was revived at the BBC in the late '80s hosted by Bob Monkhouse and then Les Dawson.

The advent of colour added greatly to the effect of light entertainment, and at a time when the "Black and White Minstrel Show" was already compulsive viewing on Saturday evenings, newly conceived programmes headlining singing stars, rather than comedy, became increasingly popular too.

Angela Rippon reveals her legs on TV for the second time, for the Royal Variety Performance, 1982. When she first danced on the Morecombe and Wise show her legs became headline news!

Although the '50s had seen, amongst others, Carol Carr's "Country Club", David Hughes' "Make Mine Music" and Joan Regans' "Be My Guest", and "The Yana Show", it was the imported Perry Como Show that had really paved the way from 1957-62 with Mr C's relaxed manner and his wealth of top rate guests and exciting choreography. The coming years were to see peak-time series starring Vera Lynn, Val Doonican (whose BBC series spanned 20 years), Rolf Harris and the Young Generation, Shirley Bassey, Cilla, Englebert Humperdinck, Petula Clark, Cliff Richard, Lulu ...

Comedy was very often an ingredient of many of these shows - Dave Allen started his very successful television career with a weekly 3-minute spot on the Doonican show, Frankie Howerd was a regular guest of Cilla. But the comedy show was starting to take on a different form in scripted programme series like "Hancock", "Steptoe and Son", Eric Sykes with Hattie Jacques, Terry and June and long running legends such as "Dad's Army", "Some Mothers Do Have 'Em", "Till Death Do Us Part", "Up Pompeii", "Are You Being Served"...

In the early '60s the 'double act' of the day was Pete and Dud (Peter Cook and Dudley Moore) who achieved much success with their filmed location sequences, studio cameos and Dud's regular music spot. These two had emerged from the Cambridge footlights revue (another source from which many great talents have been discovered).

The Frost Report brought two more characters to the notice of producers and audience alike - Ronnie Barker and Ronnie

Russ Abbot poses on his fun and games "Russ Abbot Show" for the BBC in 1990.

Corbett. But before their huge success in the next two decades with "The Two Ronnies", the '60s will always be highlighted by Morecambe and Wise, who actually had a series in the mid-'50s "Runnin' Wild" considered somewhat of a failure. But, thanks to some very inventive writing from Hill and Green, they re-emerged with much success on ATV and then later rose to greater heights and huge audiences on the BBC.

The respect they gained with artistes across the whole field of entertainment was endorsed by the broad spectrum of special guests who added extra star quality to their shows - who will ever forget the Fred and Ginger routine with Glenda Jackson, Eric's rendition of the Greig Piano Concerto with Andre Previn, Shirley Bassey's foot falling through the staircase with Eric and Ernie moving the scenery all around her, Angela Rippon's 'legs' appearing for the first time and amazing us all with her dancing ability - and so many more memorable gems of originality and comic genius.

The Frost Report also featured the talents of John Cleese, who soon teamed up with Graham Chapman, Michael Palin, Eric Idle, Terry Gilliam and Terry Jones and totally revolutionised comedy with the trend-setting "Monty Python's Flying Circus".

If not as universally successful, Tim Brooke Taylor, Graeme Garden and Bill Oddie had another major success with "The Goodies".

Whilst mentioning specialist comedy and the teams who have broken so much new ground in the last decade or so there are also some single talents that have emerged and that hold a special place in the story of television variety - one group is the impressionists.

In the '70s Mike Yarwood was uncannily convincing in the wide range of public figures and personalities he could emulate. Dick Emery and Kenny Everett (although very different in style) both created a range of characters, many with catch phrases that became household sayings, and now the tradition is carried onwards '80s style by the brilliance of Rory Bremner, Harry Enfield and Phil Cool.

In the list of 'single' talents Jasper Carrott must also rate very high with his unique ability just to sit on a stool and hold an audience.

Magicians have always been good television - in the very early days it was Jasper Maskelyne and Robert Harbin, the '50s brought us David Nixon, and of course, now Paul Daniels reigns supreme as master of the art of illusion and spectacular acts.

There are always the entertainers who are difficult to categorise. In the '70s Kenneth Williams introduced a regular run of "International Cabaret" from the talk of the town. Max Bygraves has a special place in most viewers' memories going right back for forty years; Dickie Henderson had his own series mixing his brand of comedy and dance; and Bruce Forsyth - a television star for thirty years, song and dance man and pianist, with a great sense of fun, proved to be a host par excellence of "The Generation Game" in the '70s and again in the '90s.

Since the launch of 'The Gen Game', quiz and public participation shows have been extremely popular - the list is endless "Blankety Blank", "Every Second Counts", "Bob's Full House" ... Noel Edmunds has built a big Saturday Night following with his own brand of entertainment - "The Late

Victoria Wood - As Seen on TV. The "Acorn Antiques" sketches, with Julie Walters and others, were classic send ups of soaps on TV.

Late Breakfast Show" led to his "Road Show" and now "Noel's House Party".

And what of Variety of the late '70s and '80s? There were Saturday shows on location like "Seaside Special" and "Michael Barrymore's Saturday Night Out". Alongside the marvellous "Two Ronnies" there's been comedy and conversation hosted by Des O'Conner and then Bob Monkhouse (not forgetting too the chat show of the day in the '60s hosted by Simon Dee and, of course, later large audiences had a regular date with Michael Parkinson on Saturday nights).

For the past seven years "Wogan" has had a mix of music, entertainment and conversation and introduced approximately 4,500 guests! Marti Caine mixed comedy and music. Russ Abbot and Les Dennis had big audiences for their range of comedy characters and impressions.

There's been perhaps more traditional humour from Les Dawson and Little and Large and, with the advantage on the BBC of two channels, "Not The Nine O'Clock News" has led the way to a host of other major successes - series with Rowan Atkinson, The Young Ones, Lenny Henry, Victoria Wood, French and Saunders, Stephen Fry and Hugh Laurie, Tracy Ullman, Ruby Wax, Mel Smith and Griff Rhys-Jones, John Sessions, Ben Elton, Rab C Nesbitt, KYTV ...

An amazing range of entertainment balanced currently by the other form of story-line scripted comedy represented by series like "Only Fools and Horses", "One Foot in the Grave", "'Allo 'Allo", "Birds of a Feather", "Keeping up Appearances", "Last of the Summer Wine" and many more.

Much of the variety of programmes over 50 years has also highlighted 'specials' - the 'one-off' shows that starred great international legends - Bob Hope, Jack Benny, Gracie Fields, Sammy Davis Jr., Liberace, Victor Borge and singers like Harry Belafonte, Perry Como, Tony Bennett, Jack Jones, The Beatles, Johnnie Mathis, Nat 'King' Cole, Nana Mouskouri, Barry Manilow, Tom Jones, John Denver (whose international recognition came about as a result of a BBC series after he was discovered singing in a small club in West London).

The '60s and '70s saw the best of the big bands - Duke Ellington, Ted Heath, Count Basie, Louis Armstrong, Woody Herman, Buddy Rich - and jazz reached a new and enthusiastic audience with the long running "Jazz 625". The world's leading folk artists were showcased in "Tonight in Person" and light or orchestral music was represented by the "Best of Both Worlds" featuring arranger/conductors Mantovani, Henry Mancini, Nelson Riddle, Frank Chacksfield, David Rose, Percy Faith, Stanley Black and Robert Farnon.

In the '80s "A World of Music" showcased James Galway, Harry Secombe, Kiri Te Kanawa, The King's Singers, Moira Anderson, John Williams, Jessye Norman along with many other musicians and singers who cross all musical boundaries.

There have been annual events like the Eurovision Song Contest (televised since 1960) and many awards and anniversary galas. Variety has embraced so many different forms of entertainment over the years - not to be omitted "The Good Old Days" from the City of Variety in Leeds which ran for 30 years, and the annual Royal Variety Performance, televised since the early '60s (shared annually between the BBC and ITV) has always reflected the best of the world of entertainment - in later years largely influenced by the popularity of stars known from television but in the earlier years bringing to the small screen the likes of The Crazy Gang who rarely appeared in any other television productions.

This reflection over more than 50 years is not by any means comprehensive and is only from the perspective of BBC Light Entertainment Group. Alongside all this, since 1955, ATV and then all its associate and subsequent ITV companies have, of course, also made a major contribution to the overall history of Variety on Television.

All pictures courtesy of BBC Photo Library.

THE FUTURE OF VARIETY ON TELEVISION

AN INTERVIEW WITH JOHN KAYE COOPER
CONTROLLER OF LIGHT ENTERTAINMENT, LWT

It is not a happy thought that the annual transmission of the Royal Variety Performance, alternately by the BBC and London Weekend Television, is probably the only real variety show one can see on TV in the course of the year.

Ever since the service began in 1936, right up to the eighties, Variety, in one form or another, had been part of our viewing, sometimes in an intimate cabaret format, more often direct from the stage of a large theatre like the London Palladium. Even when it began to follow the American pattern of a show hosted by a big personality, who introduced guest artistes, it was still essentially Variety. What is more, there was for many years a steady supply of new performers, introduced through the medium of such talent shows as 'Opportunity Knocks' and 'New Faces'.

What went wrong? Why is it that Variety suddenly dried up almost completely on television, despite the fact that it was often attracting audiences of over ten million? Is it, as some producers and programme controllers maintain, that light entertainment is one of the most expensive forms of television to produce and that it cannot be sold as readily in overseas' markets as drama?

John Kaye Cooper, Controller of Entertainment at LWT and a man who has spent most of his career in TV light entertainment, is not sure whether the last question applies. "Yes, it is expensive but not necessarily more so than other types of television. And I do not think it is impossible to sell British light entertainment abroad. You have only to look at Benny Hill or Dame Edna Everage.

"It may well be that we in television must take some responsibility," he says. "We are inclined to overdo things. A few years ago shows featuring impressionists were all the rage on both BBC and ITV. More recently it has been magic shows. At the moment we

Bruce Forsyth, talk shows, game shows, comedy and song and dance too!

clap clap clap clap

KEEP AN EYE ON 4

Benny Hill with dancers in the '50s. Benny was one of our most successful comedy exports.

have viewer participation shows, with ordinary members of the public telling jokes, sending in videos or displaying bizarre talents.

"I believe that everything in television, and probably in live entertainment as well, is cyclical. Somebody has an idea and everybody else copies it until every drop of originality has been squeezed out. But as far as I am concerned, 'variety' shows will always be there in one form or another. It may be shows like Barrymore, in which the star meets people in the street, and encourages anyone with talent to appear with him in their local town or city, or are invited to the studio.

"There are variations on the chat show format, like those introduced by Des O'Connor and Bruce Forsyth, in which the host talks to his guests before they perform. In recent years BBC2 and Channel 4 have specialised in finding new talent from

the comedy clubs and built shows around them - we have done it ourselves with Hale and Pace - and very occasionally we find an artiste like Richard Digance who is capable of carrying a whole show by himself with perhaps one guest performer.

"At the moment LWT is doing a new series with Brian Conley, who is perhaps the last of the generation who learnt their business in the clubs and on variety dates. Here we try to combine the traditional and the modern approach by doing the show from a theatre, allowing Brian to develop the stand-up material and sketches, with contemporary music and dance. It works with him because he is young, with great charm, uses material that rarely gives offence and, most of all, he exudes 'star quality'."

John Kaye Cooper firmly believes that the traditional style of Variety is dead, and the theatres in which it thrived have gone with it. Even their successors, the cabaret clubs, have gone as well - and those that survive can exist only at weekends using a dwindling number of headline attractions.

"Where," he asks, "are the mainstream venues?" Summer shows have largely declined to the point where they offer only short seasons by the same few star names from TV. Holiday centres offer a considerable amount of employment, but the performers, though they learn how to entertain and put across their material, can seldom rise above the level of their audiences.

What, therefore, about the so-called 'alternative' circuit? "Well, let's stop calling it 'alternative' for a start," says Cooper. "In many ways, and certainly as far as young people are concerned, it has become the mainstream. I prefer to call it New Variety or New Comedy. However, on television,

stand-up comedy is not particularly popular or effective, and when it does work it eats up material at such a rate that comedians are reluctant to do it.

"What you have to remember is that on television you need to make an immediate impact, you can't warm up the audience as you do in a theatre or club. So when you see a comedian do five minutes on television, you can be sure that it's the best five minutes he or she has got, taken out of an act that may last an hour live.

"Whether a comedian is mainstream or New Comedy, the important thing is that they make you laugh and selecting your material and learning how to perform it is a serious business. Just as in the old days of variety and the cabaret clubs, New Variety is finding its own stars who can do up to two hours on their own in comedy clubs

Michael Barrymore, a fully rounded performer, brings out the star quality of members of the public.

and sometimes theatres, but five minutes in a television show could threaten their careers.

"It is true that many of the new breed of comedians are locked into their specialist audiences and can't or don't want to become involved with the mainstream venues doing summer shows, pantomimes and the occasional cabaret club. Many of them say they don't want to be famous or appear on television. But it is largely a matter of fashion, a kind of anti-showbiz stance, and I think that this is gradually changing and that grooming is coming back.

"It was noticeable, for example, that when we did the 291 Club shows from Hackney Empire the largely Afro-Caribbean audience most appreciated those performers who had taken trouble over their appear-

ance, and this is perhaps because black entertainers have traditionally paid attention to clothes and presentation.

"I also notice a difference between performers in American comedy clubs and our own. They seem better able to bridge the gap between traditional and contemporary comedy, and there is a wider age range among their audiences. They often have better delivery, possibly because there is a

Top of page, Barrymore raises a laugh with his audience and, above, performs an hilarious 'Hell's Angel' Morris Dance on his LWT show.

The new variety star on TV, Brian Conley, shows his singing and dancing skills on his LWT show.

longer tradition of stand-up night club comedy in the States, and their subject matter is more original and varied, with a high 'recognition factor'."

But what about the talent shows, the absence of which is a greater cause of complaint from artistes, managers and agents than anything else on television? "I can appreciate the concern," replied Cooper, "because we want to find new names as much as anybody else, and realise that television is nowadays the only promotional medium for new talent.

"I myself have been actively engaged in looking for new talent ever since I went into television and have seen hundreds of acts working live in all kinds of venues and attended dozens of auditions.

"Yes, 'Opportunity Knocks' was in many ways the most effective talent show

because some winners had the opportunity to come back for several weeks so the public had the chance to get to know them. But it's not necessarily a route to stardom. What happened to Anna McGoldrick, the singer who holds the record number of consecutive weeks on 'Opportunity Knocks'?

"But in answer to those who think there are no talent shows on at the moment, I believe that there is never a time when new talent does not get its chance on television in one form or another. Barrymore, for example, may not be a talent show in the accepted sense of the word, but people new to television are on it, and the same applies to other participation shows. Ways in which we can showcase new talent are always under discussion, in the BBC and the independent companies, and a lot of formats are being brought to us.

"One of the problems is that one can devise a series and sit through literally thousands of people at auditions, but, to be honest, only a tiny proportion of those are actually good enough to go on television. When we have picked out those comparative few we are very conscious that we have got the best who are available at that time, and we have to wait three or four years before another group has developed.

"We are aware that there are hundreds of professional entertainers out there, many of whom are working regularly. But how many of them have something original to present to the viewers? Far too many singers, for instance, sing the same songs in the same style.

"Many of the comedians also lack that vital spark of originality and tell the same jokes. I find it interesting that Granada TV has recently brought back 'The Comedians' in exactly the same format as in the 1970s, and it has been well received. But it is noticeable that the best comics are nearing middle age and have years of experience

Brian Conley, sends up children's TV shows.

at telling jokes, certainly much better than ordinary viewers doing the same thing on a couple of series seen recently. So perhaps the professional joke teller will come back in fashion, because most of the New Comedy artistes don't tell jokes but deal with the comedy of observation and recollection.

"I would love to be able to do a show which would enable some of the performers discovered through talent shows to develop their style, because it is true that even if millions of people vote for an artiste as a winner of a contest, unless they get further chances on television they are soon forgotten.

"That is one of the main problems facing entertainment today, the lack of a continuing career structure of the type there was in the days of variety and, to a lesser extent, in the clubs. We can discover people and give them the chance to be seen by a huge audience, but what happens to them after that is not our concern, because we have no say in their future. Their success in the years to come will largely be due, I feel, to good management as much as their own talent, and far too many artistes have been badly advised."

The old, all-star variety shows of the 'Sunday Night at the London Palladium' and 'Live from Her Majesty's' type are in temporary eclipse, as are the 'Summertime Specials'. Here the difficulty seems to be the shortage of star names who are willing to appear on them.

"The really huge names, like Madonna, are out of our reach and in any case would insist on doing the whole show. The major pop names are not particularly interested in appearing in a variety format and would

probably not be suitable on a bill with comedians and speciality acts. So we are left with only a few stars - American singers who might be on a tour, say Diana Ross or Cher, and some British stars, such as Shirley Bassey and Tom Jones. But their availabilities are incredibly difficult to set up, especially for live shows.

"In its way, this illustrates the problems facing British show business, the decline of our own variety and club circuits, as well as summer shows, and the emergence of that vast middle ground in the mainstream sector which all too few artistes manage to cross. You could win a talent show, but that does not mean you are ready to top the bill at the London Palladium, it is just a stepping stone in your career and you still have to learn the business. But where?"

But this does not mean that light entertainment as we knew it will disappear from our screens. "Television will always come up with new formulas," says John Kaye Cooper, "and variety, although in a different form, can continue to be part of it. Sometimes it brings forth a brilliant producer, like the late David Bell, with whom I had the pleasure of working for some years. He nurtured new talent, built them into star names and transformed the look of TV Variety, bringing to it his sense of style and quality, but he also had the benefit of the golden years of Variety. We intend to go on looking and experimenting and, when the time is right, probably bringing back an old favourite or two for a new generation."

Shirley Bassey, above, and Diana Ross, top of the page, pictured when headlining on LWT Royal Variety Performances.

Pictures on pages 58 & 60 courtesy of BBC Photo Library, all others courtesy of LWT Press Stills Library.

ANIMAL TRAINING

BY SUE BOORMAN

I got involved with training animals for the entertainment industry quite by chance.

A friend of mine who has a large fruit farm locally, rang me in a panic one evening eight years ago to ask if I had a cockerel that was presentable, as she had a crew coming down the next day to film a Kelloggs' commercial. Her boys had been involved in a fight that day and were looking rather the worse for wear.

So I duly arrived the next morning clutching one of my very handsome Rhode Island Red cockerels, wondering what on earth was expected of us both. Thus my introduction into this madhat world of entertainment.

For the first couple of years I worked through agencies to get some experience, but I had so many people asking me to go freelance in the end I took the plunge. I have to say that it was the best thing I ever did.

The majority of agencies in this country act as go-betweens, between the client and animal owners, instead of training and handling which is what I do.

One of the difficult parts of filming is not so much the animals as knowing when you are needed and when you are not. Animal owners tend to be very inexperienced and extremely stage-struck which makes it very difficult to work with them and a nightmare for the crew.

A large part of animal training is common sense, the same as it is with children.

Most people in this industry that use animals are very understanding and only too ready to listen to suggestions - there is often more than one way to do something. Besides, the animals haven't always read the script!!

Although I train and handle all domestic animals, I most enjoy working with cats.

I have been involved with cats all my life, showing and breeding Burmese, with kittens exported all over the world. Cats are a nightmare to the majority of producers, they dread the word as cats are notoriously difficult to work with.

Because of this dread of using cats, there is little pressure on me as nobody expects them to do anything, so consequently the cats and I can get on and do what we were meant to be doing.

Cats are very sensitive to atmosphere and if everybody is tense about things not happening, then they never will. A splendid example of this was when I was using a cat a few years ago for a stills shot.

This particular cat had done a fair bit of work, he was a big, lazy lad and we needed a cat to lie down for this shot - just his cup of tea. No problem, I think, unfortunately the art director had a rock concert that evening that he wanted to see so he was in a rush to finish.

Could I persuade the cat to lie down? This was most definitely not on the agenda for today's performance. The photographer and I couldn't persuade the art director to leave us alone to get on with the shot.

Eventually the art director had enough and decided to go off to his concert. The cat was asleep within two minutes and the shoot was finished in ten.

The next time I worked with this art director the cat and I were left alone in peace.

I also do quite a lot of rabbit work. I trained and supplied the animals for the Beatrix Potter shoot this year in Cumbria which required wild rabbits. Some had to sit around on a hill in Cumbria which is not the easiest thing to do!

Of course, The National Trust was terrified that the rabbits would escape and repopulate Cumbria so elaborate pens had to be built to convince them otherwise.

Having sworn to the company involved that mine were tame, and wouldn't dream of making a bid for freedom, I ended up having to use some home grown, Cumbrian rabbits on the shoot as mine were too tame for the running shot.

Mine were very happy sitting on the hill but totally uninterested in the action work.

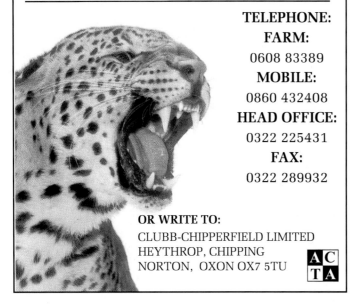
The rabbit which played Beatrix Potter's tame rabbit in the house was another story.

Whilst he was being trained, he lived in his own pen on a table by my telephone, so that when it came to filming he was perfectly adapted to the scene he was going to play.

He was used to lots of noise and movement and thoroughly enjoyed being allowed to play with all the table top accessories. He quite liked the cups of tea on offer too! Some animals are true professionals!

As I said earlier, animal training is very much a case of using common sense and encouraging the animal to do what comes naturally.

Pictures courtesy of Sue Boorman

The Sweetener that puts the others in the shade

Canderel tastes as good as sugar, and because it is made with 100% NutraSweet, unlike saccharin based sweeteners, there is no bitter aftertaste.

It is an ideal sugar substitute for those counting the calories or concerned about healthy eating. For people on the move, there are Canderel Tablets in a portable, handy size dispenser.

Alternatively there is Canderel Spoonful, available in granular form which can be used spoon-for-spoon in place of sugar. One tablet contains less than one third of a calorie, and one teaspoon of granular just two calories, compared to twenty in a teaspoon of sugar.

CANDEREL®
The star of the show

THE MANY FACES OF RUSS ABBOT

A short time ago, the Queen was visiting a shop in Norfolk. It was not an official visit, far from it. She was on holiday, staying at Sandringham and, as is her desire from time to time, she was rummaging around in the local shops, thoroughly relaxed and enjoying the experience away from the public's glaring eyes. Suddenly, she felt a gentle tug on her coat sleeve and a hand on her arm. She looked round and saw a dear old lady looking knowingly at her, a twinkle in her eye.

"I'm sorry to bother you," she said completely unaware. "It's uncanny. But you look just like the Queen. Has anyone ever told you that before?"

The Queen smiled. "How very re-assuring."

Russ Abbot has the same problem.

"I was appearing in Blackpool in summer season a few years back," he says. "It was one of those days when I had a little time to kill before the show and I really fancied some fish and chips. The more I thought about it the hungrier I became. So I popped over the road to a shop near to the theatre I knew well. It was a busy time of the day, business was brisk, and I had to wait.

"I was standing in the queue minding my own business and quietly thinking of the cod and chips that awaited me when I noticed a large lady peering through the window, pointing at me. She burst into the shop and made straight for me. She had that triumphant look of recognition on her face. I'd been spotted ...

"'Excuse me,' she said, pointing a finger. 'It is you, isn't it? It's Frank, isn't it? It is you, Frank?'

"Frank! Who's Frank?

"'Err, no,' I said almost embarrassed. 'No, No, I'm not Frank I'm urr ...'

"She reddened. 'Oh I am sorry,' she continued. 'What must you think of me. I'm looking for a friend of mine - called Frank - I can't find him anywhere. You'd know him if you saw him. He looks remarkably like Russ Abbot. Are you sure you haven't seen him?'

"She paused, a flicker of bewilderment crossed her face.

"'It's uncanny,' she was persistent. 'He looks just like you, you could be twins.'

"I stood my ground, the shop was filling up and we had created quite a scene. 'No, I'm sorry. I can't help you.'

"'Well,' she added, 'if you do see him, tell him I'm looking for him' ... and with that she was gone."

72

It's hardly surprising really. Russ Abbot has one of those faces. A raised eye-brow, a half-closed eye, a pouted mouth, a frown, a scowl ... mere gestures that from Russ can convey so much. A face that launched a thousand quips. It's a great comedy canvas on to which he paints the wide and diverse range of characters that have become his trademark. His face has certainly helped to establish him as one of Britain's best loved and most endearing comedy stars. A very funny man indeed.

Over the years, Russ Abbot's cast of comedy creations have become cult characters, adored by the public: secret agent Basildon Bond "licensed to kill and drive a heavy goods vehicle" - flying ace Boggles; the rock 'n' rolling Vince Prince; Julio Doubleglazius; Whispering Hubert; Wilf Bumworthy; Fritz Crackers; the Fat Man ... et al.

To the Chester-born comedy star, each character has been painstakingly

developed with loving care and it is this minute attention to detail that has made him (and them) so successful.

One of his first creations was called simply Boy Scout.

Says Russ: "It's funny how some characters develop, almost by accident. I was walking through the Army and Navy Store in London one afternoon when I came across a huge, outsize pair of khaki shorts on sale for just ten shillings (it shows you how many years ago it was). They looked absolutely hilarious and touched my sense of humour. I tried them on and bought them straight away.

"The next night, I wore them on stage for a joke and the audience roared with laughter.

The shorts were an instant hit, but there was nothing else I could do to develop the comic possibilities. I had no routine or funny lines to go with the outfit. Instead I made a few gestures giving an outrageous Boy Scout salute, said a few dyb dyb dybs and ended up singing a quick chorus of the old camp fire song, 'Ging Gang Gooley Gooley'.

"Before I knew it, a zany character had been born. He's been with me ever since. The funny thing is that I was never in the Scouts as a boy. However, these days, I've become honourary Akele to nearly forty different Cub and Scout troops all over the country."

Cooperman, too, has been a great favourite for many years.

"I introduced Cooperman into my act in 1978 at the time of the first Superman movie starring Christopher Reeve. I wanted to create my own typical British superhero. Originally the idea was to create a beefy, muscular character just like Christopher Reeve himself. But instead it seemed to make more sense to make him a loveable bumbler, lean and hungry, and forever getting things wrong.

"I had been a great admirer of Tommy Cooper for many years. He was my comedy hero, a madcap British comic institution. A genius. I'd been featuring an impression of Tommy in the stage act for several years, and it seemed a good idea to combine two great characters. They just clicked together. Cooperman was the result."

Yet probably the most famous and successful of all of Russ's characters is Jimmy Mac Jimmy, the orange haired Scot - See You, Jimmy.

"Ooooohtisgrooootthamafreyandstheknooall aboootmgreeeetcharacterandkinseeyouuJim myMacJimmythenoothenighhesagreetfreyu ndaminethenoonacht! D'ya ken?" as Jimmy would say.

"I am actually half Scottish," adds Russ. "It's the top half, I think, but don't tell anyone.

"My mother was born in Scotland and when I was a wee boy - I can slip into the accent occasionally - we spent many happy family holidays over the border. We used to travel up by car from Chester long before they invented motorways, so it was a long journey. Yet the closer we got to Gretna Green, the stronger my mother's Scottish accent became. Although she had been living in England for many years by then and had lost much of her native brogue, it all came flooding back to her the moment we neared the border.

"By the time we reached our destination her accent was broader than the Forth Bridge. Jimmy Mac Jimmy just developed from there. I suppose he's based on many of the people I met as a kid, relatives, friends ... but I'm not telling which. The Scots are great people, they love Jimmy and he has never offended anyone in his life."

For someone who has already guaranteed a place for himself in the annals of British comedy history and who has picked up a string of awards from his peers for his comic prowess, including Funniest Man On Television, Comedian of the Decade and Funniest Man On Television In Europe, it's hard to realise, but Russ Abbot actually had no intentions whatsoever of making his career in comedy. Far from it. His ambitions were firmly sighted on music.

No.4: THE SURE SHOT GOLF CLUB

CLASSIC

FOR THE MAN WHO THINKS THAT LITTLE BIT BIGGER

Fine Panatellas

W. D. & H. O. WILLS

5

CASTELLA

CLASSIC

MILD CIGARS

"I was drums mad," he says. "Right from an early age, all I ever wanted to do was be a drummer in a band. Nothing else mattered. Music was the big buzz. Comedy certainly never entered the frame.

"When I was fourteen, I took a part-time job at the Royalty Theatre in Chester as a stage hand working behind the scenes. And I spent many happy hours watching the shows on stage from the wings. It was here, I suppose, my formal showbusiness education began. I loved it and soon became hooked on the greasepaint. I watched all types of shows at the theatre, everything from pop concerts to the Ballet Rambert, from farce to Shakespeare, from revue to opera. There was an aura, a magical quality about it all that engulfed me.

"I was still mad keen on playing drums, though, and before long I formed my own band which later emerged as The Black Abbots, and we started playing local gigs. We were purely a pop group, playing rock 'n' roll. My life was complete more or less. I was doing something I loved and getting paid for it, well ... occasionally. Then one man, Dennis Critchley, changed it all."

Showbusiness in Britain at that time was changing. The market for live and legitimate theatre was shrinking and the Royalty, like so many other provincial theatres, was converted into one of the new breed of local theatre-cum-restaurants-cum-cabaret-clubs catering for a chicken in the basket culture that swept the country in the mid-'60s. Dennis Critchley, the Royalty's producer, could see great potential in Russ's band and offered them a contract to become the new nightspot resident group.

"We jumped at the opportunity," says Russ. "Regular work at that time was a god-send.

Once we had established ourselves, Dennis gave us a spot of our own instead of simply playing music for dancing or as the backing group to other artistes. We were a working group, but had no hit records to fall back on, much as we'd have loved to have made records. Instead we supplemented our act by adding the odd spot of comedy.

"I became the group's front man and, at that time reluctantly, the resident lunatic. Dennis was marvellous, he helped us immensely and his encouragement proved such a great grounding for me. He made me believe in myself and my ability as an entertainer, not just as a drummer. I owe him so much and it was from here that the characters slowly evolved. It started with impressions - Bruce Forsyth, Tommy Cooper - and just developed.

"The group moved on, too, and before long we were entertaining in the major working men's clubs and cabaret venues all over the north of England. Money was still very tight in those days and we travelled to and from engagements in a caravan. It made good sense. If we were booked to appear at a club for several nights at a time, we simply drove the caravan to the nearest car park and bedded down for the night. However, there were a few drawbacks.

"After one show in Middlesbrough we parked the caravan on what we thought was a plot of waste ground only to wake up the next morning to find ourselves in the middle of the town's weekly market with a hustling, bustling trade going on all around us. There were literally hundreds of people surrounding us. It was the best crowd we'd had all week.

"We never quite parked the caravan on the central reservation of the motorway, but we

came pretty close several times. But it was part of life on the road. It was a good life, too, we were young and spurred on by the dream that our big break was just round the corner and we would soon become stars."

It was.

The breakthrough for The Black Abbots came in 1969 with a series of winning appearances on television's 'Opportunity Knocks', which as Russ admits, "opened up so many doors to us." For the next ten years, the boys established themselves in no uncertain terms as one of Britain's premier comedy showgroups, topping concert, cabaret and summer season bills all over the country. They starred in their own TV specials and were rarely off the box in a heady period of success. Russ, too, was making a name for himself on television in his own right with a series of solo appearances on such shows as 'The Comedians'

and 'Who Do You Do?'. And it was because of his own rapidly emerging solo career that he decided to change his name ... and Russell Roberts became Russ Abbot.

"It was a natural progression, really," he admits. "Once I started making TV appearances on my own, I needed to establish a name of my own and an identity away from The Black Abbots. And yet the public knew me as a member of the group although my real name was rarely mentioned. I took the easy option; I resolved the problem by taking the group's name of Abbot for my own stage name. Somehow Russ Black seemed so ordinary!"

It was in 1980, however, that he decided the time was now right to branch out on his own on a permanent basis and leave The Black Abbots to go solo. His own television commitments had increased tremendously. Appearances on 'London Night Out' and 'What's On Next' had established him and he was becoming better known than the group he fronted. A decision had to be made.

"It wasn't an easy decision to make, either," says Russ. "I'd spent fifteen years with The Black Abbots. Great years. I loved working with the group. It was my life. I had security; the group was my safety net in case anything went wrong. I had the band to fall back on. It was the easy option. Yet realistically, I had nowhere to go career-wise.

"With The Abbots, I'd achieved everything I could. We'd appeared at the London Palladium, the Talk of the Town, starred in all the major clubs on many occasions. We could go no further together - just continue on the same entertainment merry-go-round. We had really reached our full potential.

"Up until that time, I had been working on a very tight schedule. Recording for television in the daytime and appearing with the group at night. Quite honestly, the strain was beginning to tell; it was becoming too much for me. Something had to give. I had a tremendous amount of TV work scheduled for the future, so I decided it would be for the best if I left the band. I agonised over the decision for ages; it was the hardest decision I have ever had to make in my life. It was an amicable split, the boys in the group were fantastic, but I was scared. Sure it was one thing to work solo on television, but a live audience was a totally different ball game.

"When I walked out on stage for the very first time on the opening night of my very own summer season in Torquay, I was physically sick, it was nauseating ... I was so nervous I could hardly speak. But as soon as the audience laughed, as soon as they warmed to me, I knew I'd made the right decision. It made sense to go solo, this was my reassurance if I'd ever really needed any."

That was the start of what has become an outstanding career for Russ Abbot.

In the years that have followed he has made the medium of television his own, headlining his own high-rating series, initially with 'Russ Abbot's Madhouse' for ITV, followed by 'The Russ Abbot Show' for the BBC. That success was consolidated with bill-topping seasons in pantomime and summer shows besides playing major provincial theatres in Britain with his record-breaking national tours.

His talent has transcended the West End stage where he scored a huge personal triumph in Neil Simon's musical comedy, 'Little Me', which ran for a year at the Prince Of Wales Theatre from the spring of 1984. It was a vehicle that seemed tailor-made for Abbot's talents at impersonation and his prowess at characterisation.

In the course of the show, he was called upon to play no less than nine crazy comedy characters, ranging from a sixteen year-old boy to an eighty year-old miser with several points in between. Three years later, he was back in the West End and another new departure, when he starred in Willy Russell's play about mid-life crisis, 'One For The Road'.

And, never one to rest on the laurels of former successes, Russ has extended his talents even further most recently by creating the role of Ted Fenwick in Granada Television's comedy drama series, 'September Son', which is as far removed as you can get from Cooperman and See You, Jimmy.

These days, however, American television audiences have taken Abbot's crazy gang of zany characters to their hearts and the

madcap comedy star is well on his way to becoming a cult character of his own Stateside.

It was in 1991 that Russ was first introduced to the American television networks when a series of shows, made up from extracts and sections taken from his successful BBC series 'The Russ Abbot Show', was sold to American television in the same way 'The Benny Hill Show' was launched on TV in the USA several years before. Since then, the Americans have been finding out what the British have known all along ... Russ Abbot is a rare breed of comedy star!

For the future, Russ admits that he would love to establish himself in the USA in the same way the late Benny Hill did. "I'd love to establish myself on an international basis," says Russ. "America is the key and I'd love to work there. But I'll never leave Britain. It's my home and I owe the British people so much."

His great ambition has remained constant since he emerged as a star in his own right: to make films. Now with the success of 'The Russ Abbot Show' across the Atlantic, his dreams could be well on the way to becoming reality in the wake of Dudley Moore, Lenny Henry and Billy Connolly.

For the time being, however, he is content to indulge himself in what he does so well, making people laugh not only in his own right, but with a little help from his crazy gang of characters.

So ... will the real Russ Abbot stand up please? ... and if you see Frank, tell him someone's looking for him.

The many faces of Russ Abbot pictured here are courtesy of Clifford Elson (Publicity) Ltd.

ODE

TO FRANK

OR
FOR A MOMENT I THOUGHT
HE WAS GOING TO MENTION MONEY

We are delighted that Barry Cryer, TV writer & personality, has allowed us to print here the personal tribute he wrote for Frankie Howerd's Memorial Service in 1992. Here are the words which Barry read to the friends and loved ones of the legend who was Frankie Howerd

Just make myself comfy ...
Once more unto the speech dear friends, once more
And sing in praise of Howerd, Francis
The tight-rope walker who always took chances
Always wobbling, never falling
Captivating and enthralling
Confiding, chiding, but never crawling
Fearful confident of his ability
Positively arrogant in his humility
Making every line a sonnet
Please yourselves - don't take a vote on it
A true friend but not a sentimental man
He was, to each lady and gentle-man
Who enjoyed his friendship which always lasted
Steadfast, never has my flabber been so gasted
I was amazed! when I realised how long it was in reality
He had beguiled us - such whimsicality
That face - someone called him King Leer and like Lear he depicted
To his audience of mad fools - a world where it was wicked to mock the afflicted
A world where pianists opined that it was chilly
With which he agreed, apparently willy nilly
While confiding to us he was sweating like a pig
Frank was always in for a penny, infra dig
He could also inform us it was bitter out
Followed by a plea to get each titter out
That we could muster - oh folly, folly!
Such irrelevance - nolle prosequi? Not on your nolle!
That face - he defined as like a milkman's horse
To which my reaction was neigh, thrice neigh, of course
Crying: "No don't laugh, it could be one of your own!"
This stand-up comedian stood alone
St Francis of Assisi - "A Sissi?" "I heard that" I can hear the retort
"How very dare you!" never was haughty quite so haught
Such haughty culture - Bottom crossed with Puck
Yet ever reminding us "Common as muck"
If that was common, may we all be so
He had common ground with us and we all know
With respect to E.M.Forster, there is no Howerd's End, that is not the case
At the risk of being naughty, shut your face
At this Eisteddfod, I shall go the whole hog
No epitaph, no epilogue. No. I joyfully conclude
The prologue.

Pictures courtesy of BBC
Photo Library

FROM THE SHIRRELL BROTHERS TO CANNON & BALL

Although Tommy Cannon and Bobby Ball are usually associated with live shows in big theatres, they are essentially products of the sixties golden era of the Northern clubs. And even though 'Opportunity Knocks' is credited as being the launching pad of many of today's big names, it quite definitely didn't work in the case of Tommy and Bobby when they appeared on the show in 1968. "The clapometer scarcely shifted," says Bobby.

They have been a professional double act for 26 years, celebrating their silver jubilee last year by starring for 25 weeks at the North Pier, Blackpool, the town in which they have had some of their greatest successes. But they have known each other for more than 30, when they met on Tommy's first day at work in an Oldham engineering factory; Bobby, still in his teens, had been employed there for some time as a welder. Tommy, in his early twenties, had tried several jobs but his real ambition was to be a singer and, after doing a double act with his sister Mavis, was working solo in the clubs.

Bobby fancied show business as well but had contented himself with making his workmates laugh and becoming one of the most popular lads in the factory. Tommy recalls, "It was my first day in a new job and as I went to clock in this chirpy little bloke came up to me and said, 'How are ya, cock?' gave me a big grin, put his arm round my shoulder and took me in to meet the other lads. We were pals for life from that moment on."

Odd really, because Bobby, the natural clown of the works, thought Tommy, over five years older, was tall, suave and sophisticated but, as often happens, apparent opposites achieved a natural rapport. Before long, Tommy discovered that his mate Bobby could charm a club audience with singing. By the end of the night their minds were made up - they would become a double act.

Thus was formed the Shirrell Brothers, later the Harper Brothers, Harper being Bobby's real name. As a vocal duo they played as semi-pros in clubs throughout Lancashire for two years, sometimes getting £10 a night between them, occasionally working for a couple of pints and a meat pie, while still keeping their jobs at the factory - "not much fun when we didn't get home until 2 or 3 a.m. and had to clock on at 6 a.m.," laughs Tommy.

Eventually came the time when they knew they ought to make the plunge towards full-time professionalism, being pushed into it when they were told off for rehearsing their act on the factory floor. "It was an agent who said we ought to think seriously about turning pro," says Bobby, "so that was the opportunity. We decided to call ourselves Cannon and Ball, mainly because

we were beginning to put more comedy into the act and we thought we ought to have a name to match. Tommy decided to call himself Cannon because he, being an old rocker, liked the American singer Freddie Cannon. So I had to become Ball because it went with Cannon."

The first months as pros were fairly disastrous. So, far from becoming stars overnight, Tommy and Bobby worked an average of one night a week, concentrating mainly on singing. They failed three auditions for 'Opportunity Knocks' before finally making that inauspicious debut, which prompted them to turn the act round to put the emphasis on comedy.

From then on Tommy and Bobby never looked back. From playing the small social and working men's clubs they rapidly progressed to the major venues of the day, the cabaret clubs that offered full-week bookings, such as the Batley Variety Club, to which they returned year after year, winning all the clubland awards that were going.

But, despite the success that enabled them to buy houses and cars and to provide for their families, theirs was essentially regional fame. For national recognition they had to wait until the end of the seventies, the man responsible for their breakthrough being the late David Bell, who had been brought down from Scotland to head up the light entertainment side of London Weekend Television.

Bell was anxious to find new faces to put into his ambitious Saturday night entertainment 'Brucie's Big Night,' starring Bruce Forsyth. The format he adopted for Cannon and Ball was to slot them into the show with six comedy sketches, and although

the production, perhaps ahead of its time, was brilliantly publicised, and the public was told to look out for the great new comedy act, Tommy and Bobby were devastated to discover that not one of their sketches was actually used in the ill-fated series.

But David Bell, confident in the abilities of his discoveries, did manage to fit them into a spot with an excerpt from their club act into the Christmas edition and they became an instant hit with the viewers, so much so that they were immediately offered a series of their own beginning in the spring of 1979.

Then bad luck struck again. After only one show had been transmitted, and Bobby's red braces and "Rock on, Tommy" had become part of the national consciousness, the ITV technicians began a three-month strike and they were off the air again. "We couldn't have been more depressed," recollects Tommy. "After all that publicity and the tremendous success of our first two TV appearances, we disappeared again - the act that never was!"

At last things began to turn their way. The series was eventually screened in the following autumn and shot to the top of the ratings. What's more, it was immediately followed by a second series made while the first was being transmitted, giving them 12 weeks of practically continuous exposure on the small screen.

In 1980 came the first of what would be a run of phenomenally successful summer seasons, and in the town upon which they had set their ambitions nearly 20 years earlier, Blackpool, mecca of summer entertainment. During that first season they played to a staggering 98 per cent capacity and, unfortunately, one fan died in his seat laughing. His widow later wrote to the boys begging them not to feel guilty "That's the way he would have liked to have gone," she explained.

They had another tremendous success five years later in Blackpool, this time at the much larger Opera House, which they filled for ten weeks. By this time they had become established as pantomime stars as well, playing to over 2 million in their debut season at the London Palladium and creating the biggest box office gross in a single week in the history of British theatre.

Since then they have diversified in other directions, making a film, 'The Boys in Blue', which has done astonishingly well on video rental. They have toured in a farce, 'You'll Do For Me', and, getting away from their usual brand of TV comedy,

became quiz show hosts in 'Cannon and Ball's Casino' and starred in a situation comedy series, 'Plaza Patrol'.

But one suspects that they are at their happiest on stage, facing a live audience and getting the kind of charge that only the sound of laughter can bring. But they do have an ambition to be recognised as singers as well as comedians, for that is how they started, and they never neglect the chance to put in a few songs in their stage shows.

Unlike many artistes, they are not show business fanatics, just waiting for the moment to get on stage. Tommy is a golfer of some renown in showbiz circles, owns and rides his own horses and has run a professional football club.

Bobby is more interested in business, having had an interest in a club and running his own recording studio, though he also writes poetry and created a series of children's characters called Juniper Jungle, which have turned into books and videos. Both his sons are also keen on music and show business, Robert as a comedian, Darren as a singer-songwriter.

And in case you might be wondering how it came about that Bobby wears an ill-fitting suit and those red braces on stage, it is because he bought his first stage suit in an Oxfam shop for £5, took it home and found it was much too large, used a belt to hold the baggy trousers up and then took Tommy's advice and wore braces instead. Like many comedy trademarks, this one began by accident - but now he wears tailor-made baggy suits and twangs his way through 50 pairs of red braces a year.

Pictures courtesy of
Cannon & Ball's agent.

DICK EMERY –
AN APPRECIATION, BY PETER ELLIOTT

I first met Dick Emery in the summer of 1959 when I was doing a double act with the late Marty Feldman, who was also writing at the time a TV and radio show called 'Educating Archie'.

Dick had a small part in the show which also starred, apart from Peter Brough and Archie Andrews, Max Bygraves. We got on quite well and had a similar sense of humour, but it was not until the winter of

1966 when Dick and I met up again at the New Theatre, Cardiff in a pantomime in which he was playing the leading role of Mother Goose, and I was one of the brokers men together with my partner Jimmy Edmondsen. I also had a broken leg which I had unfortunately sustained in a car accident in the summer of 1966.

When I turned up at the theatre for rehearsals in Cardiff with my right leg in

plaster, supporting myself with two sticks, the management were, to say the least, unhappy. Dick however, said "Oh, no problem, Peter can play the part of the village idiot," and we went to the wardrobe and he sorted out a large smock which covered me down to the calves of my legs, an old hat with straw in it and a staff which enabled me to walk on and off the stage.

From that moment our friendship was cemented and, when my partner retired from show business some two years later, I joined Dick and we worked together as an act for some years, and I eventually became his manager.

His success of course is now known worldwide. As a character actor I would say that he ranked with some of the best in the world, he was also a fine front cloth comic, mimic, singer and could also write and direct.

The talent never seemed to stop from this man, who was small in stature but extremely high in his theatrical achievements.

His death was a great loss to the theatre generally and television in particular and I consider myself extremely lucky to have been his friend for so many years.

Some of the many faces of the multi-talented Dick Emery. All Emery pictures courtesy of the BBC from the series Emery - Legacy of Murder, except picture on page 89, which is courtesy of Peter Elliott.

BILLY DAINTY -

AN APPRECIATION, BY LEN LOWE

The moment Billy Dainty and I were brought together in 1967 we hit it off professionally. We had known each other for years, of course, because your paths cross in this business.

I started in the business as a child actor, appearing in West End shows like Cavalcade at Drury Lane, then I joined Jack Hylton's band in 1934 and after the war was half of the double act Len and Bill Lowe. Billy was a bit younger and never got started until after the war, when he was a dancer in West End and touring shows before he decided to take up comedy. He was always a bit on the chubby side for a dancer.

We just found ourselves booked for the same show in 1967 - Stanley Willis-Croft was the producer - Billy as the comedian, me as the straight man and singer and within hours, or so it seemed, it felt as if we had always been working together.

We never intended to be a double act and in many ways we weren't, because we lived separate lives offstage and were known in the business as individuals with years of experience between us. But some-how we clicked from the outset, perhaps just because we knew what was required, what would work and what wouldn't.

We had that kind of telepathy that you find in all the best double acts. It's based on good solid experience but leaves a lot of

room for improvisation and ad-libbing, so that as the straight man I somehow sensed what Bill was going to do next. All the great double acts have this gift of course, but they probably developed it over a long period of time working together, whereas Bill and I just fell into it naturally.

We certainly had lots of laughs together, particularly when we were persuaded to go into the clubs, because that's where the money was in the late sixties. We were essentially stage performers, brought up on the discipline of variety, in which all the moves were plotted and the acts were timed to the last minute and the greatest sin was to overrun.

In the clubs, though, you were expected to do time, anything up to an hour, and Bill was terrified. "I've never done more than twelve minutes in my life," he said when we got to our first job and found we had to do more like 45.

It was at the Tranmere Rovers Social Club in Birkenhead, I believe, and we were even more put out when we discovered that instead of the orchestra we were used to we found that the accompaniment consist-ed of a three-piece rock and roll group, none of whom could read music.

We had carefully prepared an act of miscel-laneous bits and pieces, comedy cross-talk, songs and dances, and more or less had to throw the whole lot out of the window. I

remember that when we came to Billy's cod ballet, always one of the highspots of his act, I actually had to sing the music because the band hadn't the first idea of how to play it. Of course, it wasn't all like that.

Eventually we discovered what club audiences liked and gave it to them and we always took the trouble to find out what the musicians were like before we accepted the booking. Some of them weren't too

Dainty takes part in a routine for the 1982 Royal Variety Performance.

back on the stage, where we felt we belonged. Twenty years ago there were more summer seasons than there are nowadays and we did some nice ones at places like the Cliffs Pavilion, Southend, when they could still muster 12 dancers and a decent sized orchestra and Bill was really at his best.

And of course he really was one of the great pantomime dames, cheeky and charming and getting the most out of every line. What's more he had that agility and the knack of satirising feminine characteristics without giving offence.

Somewhere, deep down, I sensed that Billy was quite a serious man who took his business very seriously. He came from Dudley and when he was a boy went to Betty Fox's famous dancing school in Birmingham. She supplied juveniles to the leading pantomimes in the Midlands but Billy was actually quite keen on classical ballet.

bad so we were able to put in more of the stage act, but it was often a bit of a knife - edge job, what with some audiences being much noisier than others.

I remember once that we were having a terrible time at one club and Billy had worked himself into the ground trying to make them laugh. He had done all his verbal comedy bits, all the funny walks and falls - and then, to cap it all, his small dental plate with his front teeth on it fell out on to the stage, which got the biggest laugh of the night. But Bill wasn't bothered - he tore off the little hairpiece which covered his bald patch and shouted "You've seen it all now!", and stalked off.

In many ways they were great days, but I must admit we were always pleased to get

When he was 15, though, he came up to London to take tap and modern dancing lessons from the great Buddy Bradley, which is how he got to be in West End shows. He was in "Piccadilly Hayride" at the Prince of Wales with Sid Field, you know, and then went into a show with Cicely Courtneidge in the West End, so he had a good grounding in classy productions.

Despite his funny face and great all-round talent for humour, there was always something quite classy and distinctive about Billy. He was never your conventional variety comic. From the beginning he attracted quite an intelligent following, rather like Max Wall I suppose, because of his originality, and that is why I think he is remembered today.

He was never quite a star in the accepted sense of the word, despite the success of his later television programmes. In a lot of shows he was actually the second comic, often to Harry Worth, and I don't think he ever strove towards stardom.

I think Billy was a bit upset when he realised he was never going to be a star dancer because that was originally his ambition. "I'd give anything to be like Gene Kelly," he told me more than once, "that's who I call a real star." A bit later he fancied himself as a romantic singer, with a particular leaning towards Tony Bennett, and in fact he once made a record. But he knew well enough that comedy was his forte and that his build was against him

becoming either a graceful dancer, though he did have his own kind of grace, or a romantic singing idol.

I look back on the seven years we spent working together as the highspot of my long professional life, because he was a generous performer, always at his happiest and best when in a company.

Although Bill was naturally a very funny man, I don't think he would have been entirely at home in today's comedy environment, when young comedians have to work alone of necessity, doing one-nighters most of the time. He liked the big theatres, the lights and the music - and the company of his fellow artistes, the family feeling of the business, if you like.

He was loyal and lovable - he had the same agent, first Lillian Aza, then her son Morris, practically throughout his career. This was the same agent as Roy Hudd, of course, so they naturally came together towards the end of his life in the show "Just a Verse and Chorus", in which they both paid tribute to the business of the past.

He had a real feeling for the business and for the welfare of its members, which is why, like myself, he played an active part in the affairs of the Grand Order of Water Rats. I believe that everybody who ever worked with him misses him very much, because not only was he a lovely chap but we can still visualise his appearance and his act, which was an undoubted classic.

As a comedian I can sum him up by saying that some comics say funny things, but Billy Dainty said ordinary things in a sublimely funny way.

All pictures courtesy of the BBC
Photo Library

THE LIFE & TIMES OF
JIM DAVIDSON

Jim Davidson's showbusiness career was over at thirteen! Before he had time to blossom in the world of entertainment, his career had gone, nipped in the bud. All washed up after less than two years in the business.

"Yeah," says the Blackheath-born comedian "I was thirteen and totally disillusioned with showbusiness when I was turned down for the role of 'Artful Dodger' in the film version of Lionel Bart's musical, Oliver. Jack Wild got the part instead. That was it. I quit. I'd had enough."

To be quite truthful, Jim's showbusiness career had actually only started a handful of months before.

"I had my first taste of entertaining on a grand scale when I was twelve with Ralph Reader's Gang Show at the Golders Green Hippodrome," he admits. "It came about by accident, like so much of my career. I've been very lucky.

"I was on holiday with my parents in Norfolk at the time, when my father met a guy who said he was associated with Ralph Reader and had connections with the Gang Show.

"He must have been taken with me because he asked me if I'd like to audition for the show. Well ... being a Boy Scout myself, a member of the 25th Blackheath Troop, I knew all about the Gang Shows.

They were a bit special with the scouts and to appear in the actual show at Golders Green was a great honour. I jumped at the chance.

"Looking back, it's quite amazing really. I auditioned for Ralph Reader himself on stage at ... *the London Palladium*. Can you imagine it? Performing on the 'world's greatest stage' at twelve. Some entertainers only dream about appearing at the Palladium and go through an entire career without ever making it. And here was I, not even a teenager, walking out on to that revered stage. It was incredible; a great feeling, but I think I was a bit too young to appreciate it then. Still, I must have impressed Ralph Reader because I got the job.

"At that time, I wasn't bad at impressions. Besides impersonating most of my teachers - much to their annoyance - and a few friends and neighbours, I was quite good at taking off the odd TV character. Ralph Reader liked that idea, so as well as appearing in the show as part of the chorus, performing in all the big production numbers, I was given a six-minute spot of my own, telling gags and doing impressions. That was in 1966 just after England won the World Cup. I must have been quite good because I was invited to appear in the show the following year and really felt that showbusiness was just the job for me. It wasn't like working for a living. Then ... I came down to earth when I was over-looked for Oliver. No-one told me it was also a hard life!"

So Jim had to go back to the more mundane things in life like going to school (Kidbrooke Park Junior Middle School and St. Austen's School, Charlton) where he was already renowned as "something of a lad and a bit of a comedian" even then. He often skipped lessons to go fishing and spent most of his spare time by a river bank, or on the side of a gravel pit, or canal. He caught a record 28 1/2 lb pike when he was sixteen. That was the first of many occasions, too, and he's rarely been out of the newspapers ever since. Music was another great passion and at about the same time, he started playing drums and teamed up with a piano player and they entertained together in local pubs.

He left school shortly afterwards and set about finding a suitable job to occupy his days, and make him a few bob into the bargain.

"I had quite a few jobs," he admits sheepishly. "You name it, I did it: messenger, truck driver, window cleaner, porter, painter, decorator, driver. I kept getting the sack because I couldn't get up in the morning. I was always late for work. Can you imagine it? I even took a job as a milkman which nearly killed me. Getting up in the middle of the night to go to work was crazy. It wasn't my idea of fun. That was a great mistake. Suffice to say the job didn't last very long - two days I think, and I suppose I must have gone through three or four jobs each month."

Then - again by accident - his showbusiness career was given the kiss of life. "My mates and I used to frequent a pub in Woolwich that put on entertainment most Sunday evenings. They often had a band playing or a stand up comedian. It was a way of attracting punters. In pubs across London there was a thriving entertainment scene. Anyway, on one particular Sunday evening, we arrived at the pub only to find that the comedian hadn't

turned up which was a great disappointment. We'd only gone along to see the act. Then somehow my friends persuaded me to get up and tell a few gags. Well ... encouraged by a few speedy 'halves' and the shouts of the crowd, I took the bait. Typical! And I ended up on stage doing a makeshift act of sorts, trying desperately to remember all the gags I knew. But it worked. The audience loved it and the more they laughed and shouted encouragement, the more confident I grew. In the end, I thoroughly enjoyed myself and I got a good reception.

"After that I had this great desire to make people laugh. That was how it all started. From there I used to appear as often as I possibly could in pubs and clubs throughout South London; the more confidence I gained, the more work I got and the better known I became. My mother used to ring up the pubs and clubs and pretend to be my agent. She asked them if they wanted to book this young, up-and-coming comedian.

"After about six months in the business, I landed a residency at the Black Bull public house in Lewisham. It was a notable step in my career. I'd actually been recommended to the landlord who wanted to see me. I spun him a line about all the places I'd appeared in the past, and he bought it - offered me a regular engagement at the grand sum of £6.00 a spot.

"Before long, I was working virtually every night as a comic and making a good living, too, although I was still officially only semi-professional. However, when I got the sack from my latest day job, I decided to turn it in and determined to make showbusiness my career. I haven't had what you would call a 'proper' job since."

Sallmanns' recent curtain raiser has only been so successful due to the help and assistance of our many friends.
Our thanks in particular to the following stars:

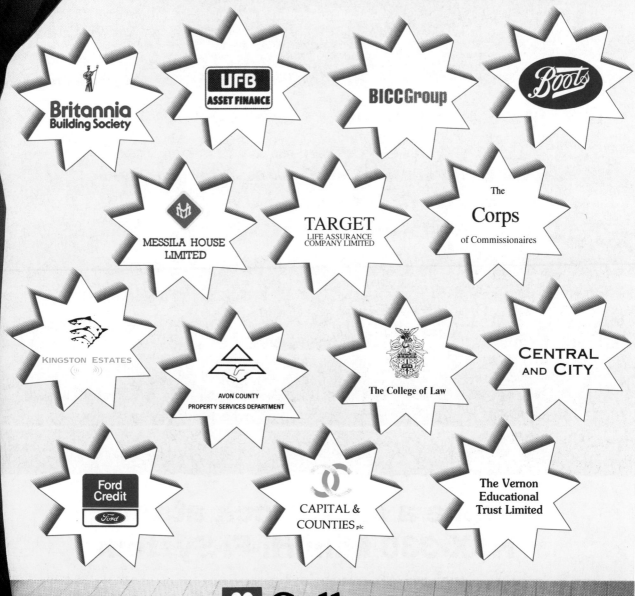

Sallmanns

INTERNATIONAL PROPERTY CONSULTANTS

211 PICCADILLY, LONDON W1V 9LD. Telephone: 071 409 2222 Fax: 071 895 1375

Take a closer look at the NSX-330 Mini Hi-Fi System

Impressive as it is elegant, the **NSX-330** has a wealth of powerful features that combines the most advanced technology with the ultimate in operation convenience; **AI (Artificial Intelligence) Navigation** reduces the number of controls overall – only one set is shared by the Tape deck, Tuner and CD Player. You are then guided by LEDs on the buttons to the ones which can be used in a particular mode.

As a result, the NSX-330 becomes much easier to operate, leaving you, the listener, to fully appreciate its other stunning features: • **BBE High definition sound** • **Super T-Bass** • **Fully programmable CD Player** • **30 watts per channel (1% THD RMS) Amplifier** • **Full Remote Control** • **32 Station random pre-set Tuner** • **Dolby B Noise Reduction** • **Twin auto-reverse Cassette Deck** • **3-way high performance loudspeakers.**

All this and more for only £299.99*

For more information and details of your local dealer please phone: 081 897 7000

aiwa
DIGITAL AUDIO & VIDEO

And I had that desire." 'New Faces' in 1976 proved to be his big breakthrough.

"It's hard to believe it, but I passed the audition for 'New Faces' doing exactly the same act as the one with which Hughie Green rejected me on 'Opportunity Knocks'," says Jim. "It was a crazy situation."

'New Faces' was the show on which the general public discovered for the first time, Jim's long-standing catchphrase, 'Nick! Nick!' and took it (and him) to their hearts.

Says Jim: "I didn't really invent the catchphrase, 'Nick! Nick', I borrowed it. Where I lived, whenever a policeman was spotted coming into view by the other kids, they yelled out: 'Nick! Nick!' I suppose it was a kind of warning - look out, the cops are about." Jim didn't win the show's Grand Final. He came second to Roger de Courcey and Nookie Bear, yet the impact he made on television was immediate. It launched an outstanding career.

TV proved the ideal medium for the comedy star and he consolidated his early success with appearances on such series as 'What's On Next', 'On Net', 'Seaside Special' and 'London Night Out' among many, before he was given a series of his own, 'The Jim Davidson Show' in 1979. The same year he returned to the stage of the London Palladium to appear in the Royal Variety Show.

'The Jim Davidson Show' ran for five series on ITV and gained for its star the award as Funniest Man On Television.

Throughout the 1980s, Jim extended his talents further to prove he was more than just a stand up comedian, by starring in

By the mid-1970s, Jim Davidson was emerging as a very funny comedian. His machine-gun style and cheeky sense of humour endeared him to many people wherever he appeared. He was well known in most parts of London, particularly around his own stamping ground in the south. But good as he was, his success was still only limited; he needed to branch out to establish his name nationally if he was to stand any chance. The next obvious step was television.

Jim auditioned for Hughie Green's 'Opportunity Knocks' on ITV and was turned down. Yet this time instead of giving up and finishing with showbusiness for good as he had done not ten years before, the experience gave him a greater determination to succeed. "To be a good comedian, you need a great desire to be loved.

two successful situation comedy shows: 'Up The Elephant And Round The Castle' (4 series) followed by 'Home James' (4 series) for which he created the roguish-yet-loveable character of 'Jim London', ironically a sort of latter-day 'Artful Dodger'. Most recently, his TV career has diversified even more to embrace the hit quiz shows, 'Big Break' and 'Jim Davidson's Treasure Island'.

Jim Davidson's career has not only been confined to the realms of the small screen. He has built a vast reputation for himself in live theatre. Pantomime has played its part, too, and Jim has appeared in many including two in the West End. In 1980, he starred in 'Dick Whittington' at the London Palladium, and in 1991 played Buttons in 'Cinderella' at the Dominion Theatre.

Early in his career, he endeared himself in no uncertain terms to British cabaret audiences and carved a huge name for himself in clubland. At one time, he was one of only a handful of British entertainers whose very name alone could guarantee to pack nightspots wherever he played, anywhere in the country, and as such, he was very much in demand. Recently with the decimation of the British club scene, Jim has turned to the theatre where he reigns supreme.

In an age that has seen showbusiness dominated by a brand of comedy and humour that is termed alternative; where new style comedians have cornered the market leaving traditional comedy stars branded old fashioned and out of vogue, Jim Davidson's own reputation has remained very much untarnished by this new-wave attack.

Indeed, he remains a brilliant stand up comedian in his own inimitable right, in a class of his own and certainly unchallenged

by this new breed, as one of the funniest men in British showbusiness. He regularly tours the country in his own outrageous, adults-only show, 'An Evening With Jim Davidson', which is one of the most talked about shows in the business, often for the wrong reasons. It has been decried and criticised unmercifully by some local authorities in some of the towns in which it has played. And yet, the general public have registered their own feelings on the subject by packing theatres everywhere. As a measure of that success, in 1992 'An Evening With Jim Davidson' completed a record-breaking third consecutive summer season - back by outstanding public demand - at the Princess Theatre, Torquay. It also marked its fifth season at the theatre in six years.

"These days I like to go out on stage without having any pre-set routines," says Jim. "I like to get the feel for an audience and react to them. I like to talk to them, which is a great source of inspiration. I can come out with whatever comes into my head. In that way no two evenings on stage are ever the same and the act is always different; always fresh. No-one, least of all me, knows from night to night what I'm going to say."

Although Jim has a reputation for being a "man's comic", a large proportion of his audience is made up of women.

"Despite all the criticism from some quarters saying that I'm sexist, women seem to enjoy my act enormously; I am very popular amongst the ladies," smiles Jim.

"Let's face it, most women laugh at the same things men laugh at, but they'll never admit to it. They try to act all prim and proper - but when they are in a crowd, all girls together, they really let their feelings known. There's no stopping them. Women like to be shocked and I've done my fair share of that over the years with my act, thinking about things they wouldn't normally discuss in the open, or certainly not in mixed company. Women like to let their hair down occasionally and, like us fellas, have a good laugh. But I rarely offend the ladies. How could I. I love 'em all, that's been my trouble. How could I upset them?"

Another section of the community Jim has a very special affinity to is the Armed Forces. Over the years he has gone out of his way to perform shows for British servicemen and women stationed overseas, travelling to such far away places as Belize in Central America. He regularly appears in Germany - one such visit was filmed for a highly entertaining Christmas TV special, 'Jim Davidson In Germany'. He has also completed several tours of duty to the South Atlantic entertaining in the Falkland Islands. In 1985, 'Jim Davidson's Falklands Special', screened on ITV, told the story of one such sortie.

"Servicemen and women do a terrific job for us all," says Jim. "I'm very proud of them. We owe them a lot, too. So I'm more than happy to do my bit for them ... and give something back. If I can bring a little laughter into their lives for the service they have given us, then that's tremendous. They're great people." They think the world of Jim, too.

Giving back is something Jim knows all about. Since he started out in showbusiness he has raised many hundreds of thousands of pounds through his own personal appearances, or by organising special shows, or by laying on Midnight Galas, for numerous charities, including the Sharon Allen Leukemia Trust, of which he is a very active chairman. It's a part of his life he rarely talks about, he just gets on with it and does it with great effect.

Jim Davidson & John Virgo enjoying their work on the BBC' Big Break.

These days, however, Jim is combining a career as an entertainer with that of a successful businessman - the proud owner of his own audio and sound company, Alpha Audio, supplying equipment to showbusiness. It's a role he relishes.

"I love it," he admits. "It's great to be involved with something so totally different to what I do on stage. It's certainly opened up a whole new world of technology to me."

And for the first time in over twenty years, Jim Davidson has at last found himself a proper daytime job he actually likes doing.

Pssst ... and he's never late for work.

IT'S NO JOKE

Life for a successful businessman can be very rewarding but the attention of the Tax Inspector can make financial rewards (at least) 40% less attractive.

"Please call to see me so that we can discuss your accounts".

These days the taxman does not always write - he may just turn up on the doorstep. You can not laugh it off but equally you should not panic.

The impact of a tax enquiry can be felt not just on your wealth but also on your health. How do you cope with the strain of having someone assess the accuracy of your financial statements and pry into your business? How do you defend yourself against the threat of public exposure and a possible criminal record?

The real need is for considered advice at an early stage and, if it comes to investigation, professional support.

If the Tax Inspector is satisfied, there is always Customs and Excise to consider. VAT is common tax throughout the European Community and needs to be considered whenever and wherever a service is performed. It is a fairly safe bet that VAT will be chargeable somewhere on services in the EC, even if they are not VATable in UK terms.

"The specialist team at Avari & Associates", says Noshir Avari "can boast over 200 years total work inside the Revenue and Customs Department in direct and indirect tax and investigations. We look after entertainers, local authorities, travel agents, builders, engineers, caterers, stockbrokers - whatever your speciality we have a team for you. A fast, personal service is our guarantee. Quality is our hallmark. Value for money is ensured because we guarantee to fix a fee at the start - we don't ask for a blank cheque for costs".

When our work is finished you can even tell your friends about the funny side.

....

**For all your specialist tax needs, call
the Avari team from the outset:**

NOSHIR AVARI

DAVID TUNNEY   **BRIAN TOLL**   **DUNCAN GROVES**
Companies   VAT   PAYE

217 Kings Road   Harrow   Middlesex   HA2 9LF
✳ **Tel 081 864 5315**   ✳ **Fax: 081 864 1025**

LES DAWSON AN APPRECIATION

BY JOHN SMERIN

" One night I just sat there gazing at the night sky, and I saw the myriad of stars glisten like pieces of diamond thrown carelessly over black velvet. In awe I watched the waxen moon ride across the zenith towards the ebb and void of infinite space, wherein the tethered boats of Jupiter and Mars hang forever festooned in their orbital majesty. And I remember thinking through all this - I must put a roof on this lavatory!"

Well designed images leading ever-expectantly to a crippling back-to-earth punchline, and all delivered in a disdainful throw-away Northern monotone, can only be attributed to one man, comedian Les Dawson.

With Ken Dodd probably now the only top-liner remaining of those great comics weaned on the long-since defunct variety stages, Les Dawson can now be considered one of the founding fathers of the stand-up comics of the last 30 years who served their apprenticeships in the working men's clubs of the late '5Os and early '60s.

The 'bon-mot' and the carefully turned phrase is much more of the Dawson stock-in-trade than the mere telling of a joke or funny story. He is a wordsmith with several books and novels already to his credit.

"I enjoy words" Les has said,"Not big words just for the sake of using them like some people do. The English language is full of funny words and phrases, if you use them right .
Les Dawson had in fact started out after the war with the intention of becoming a writer. He went to Paris for this purpose, but ended up playing piano in a bar. The bar was always strangely empty until he gradually realised that the whole scene was actually a mere front for the activities taking place on an upper floor. "I think I was only there to make up the rhythm pattern."

Back home, Les embarked on various unsuccessful entrepreneurial activities culminating in 'Garden Fantasia', a garden accessories business - gnomes and the like. But by then he was supplementing his dwindling income with stand-up work in working men's clubs, the first being in Middleton, Manchester for 25 shillings.

What audience there was must have been comprised of undertakers. "I guessed that," said Les, "for they brought their clients with them." To give himself courage, Les started drinking at 5.30 and minutes after he got on stage he fell right off it again.

Enough bookings followed to tempt him to try it full time - or perhaps it was sheer desperation. But the years that followed were extremely hard ones for Les Dawson even though he was building on experience and an act that was eventually to serve him well.

Personifying the national spirit, Les as John Bull, from his '80s series 'The Les Dawson Show" for the BBC

One of his favourite 'one-liners' stems from this period of austerity in the clubs. Les remembers an act where a man walked across a wire, 4 foot above the stage, made a 'very half hearted' cartwheel and exited pulling a face. He did this without a word for three nights. On the Thursday according to Les, the man 'snapped'. While walking along the wire he suddenly stopped and turning to face what laughingly passed for an audience ("a few white blobs scattered here and there") he said, 'D'you know, you can walk along here somedays and never see a soul'. Les Dawson has used that actual line many times himself at the start of his act since then, and he has made the 'god-only-knows-what-I'm-doing-here' attitude his own to great effect.

During those years, however, he must have wondered many times what he really was doing here. Yet to this day he never decries the working mens' club background or those hard years. With variety changing, these were the only outlets whereby a comic could learn his trade and adapt his act.

But hard years they were, and Les will always remember the Christmas dinner of 1960 which he and his newly-pregnant wife shared consisting of one egg apiece.

Inevitably the slogging paid off, and with a chance on TV in 'Comedy Band Box' with David Nixon and a discovery by Hughie Green on 'Opportunity Knocks', Les Dawson finally became an 'overnight success'.

The Les Dawson brand of comedy has kept well away from politics, religion and the other trappings of today's alternative humour. Yet the changing scene of modern life and particularly the woman's role has brought Les an abundance of criticism over his own sources of material, namely 'the wife' and the 'mother in law', culminating inevitably in the mantel of King of Male Chauvinists being placed firmly on his shoulders.

But he has always shrugged it off. "It is merely a defence mechanism," he has explained "And if people would care to listen, they would realise that in every situation I give myself, I'm always the one who comes off worse".

His own family, he has insisted, has never taken objection to any of his on-stage remarks. The 'mother in law' joke is one of the oldest and most original in history, so Les's research has it..

It dates back to Roman times where a centurion says to one of his cohorts, "Why dost thou wish to spend thine hours in Britain?" "To see the mother in law." "But she lives surely in Vesuvius" "Yes, I know, but she looks better from Britain".

Les in curlers for the BBC's "The Dawson Watch" transmitted in 1980.

Les Dawson would then go on to explain that his own mother in law was, in fact, the first person to hear that particular story. But all the time he would insist that in reality she is a wonderful person.

"There was that time a few years back," Les has said, "When skate boards were all the rage. One of these kids was coming towards me on a skate board, and just like a child, wasn't looking where he was going. He would really have hurt my ankle if it wasn't for the mother in law who had the presence of mind to throw me under a bus!"

In truth, Les's attitude towards marriage and the family are much more respectful than suggested from his on-stage persona. His first marriage was a very close one and his nursing of his wife during her last years of acute illness was very much to the detriment of his own health and career. His second marriage, to Tracy, has blossomed over the last couple of years, although she in turn has had to

Good direct mail can also be touched, smelt, heard, even kicked around the room.

In fact, direct mail is totally versatile. It can be just about any size, weight or shape.

It can be a single item or an elaborate presentation.

But there is one thing that's hard to do with it, if it's been properly targeted.

That's bin it.

Over five hundred thousand* people who reply to direct mail every week testify to that.

For more information about direct mail, write to Neville Holland, Royal Mail, FREEPOST, LONDON EC2B 2BB or telephone on 0800 900 965.

NAME MR/MRS/MS

JOB TITLE

COMPANY

ADDRESS

POSTCODE

PHONE   TE1K

If you'd like one of our account managers to contact you, tick here. ☐ If you do not wish to receive information on other Royal Mail products and services, please tick here. ☐

DIRECT MAIL

*Source: Direct Mail Information Service.

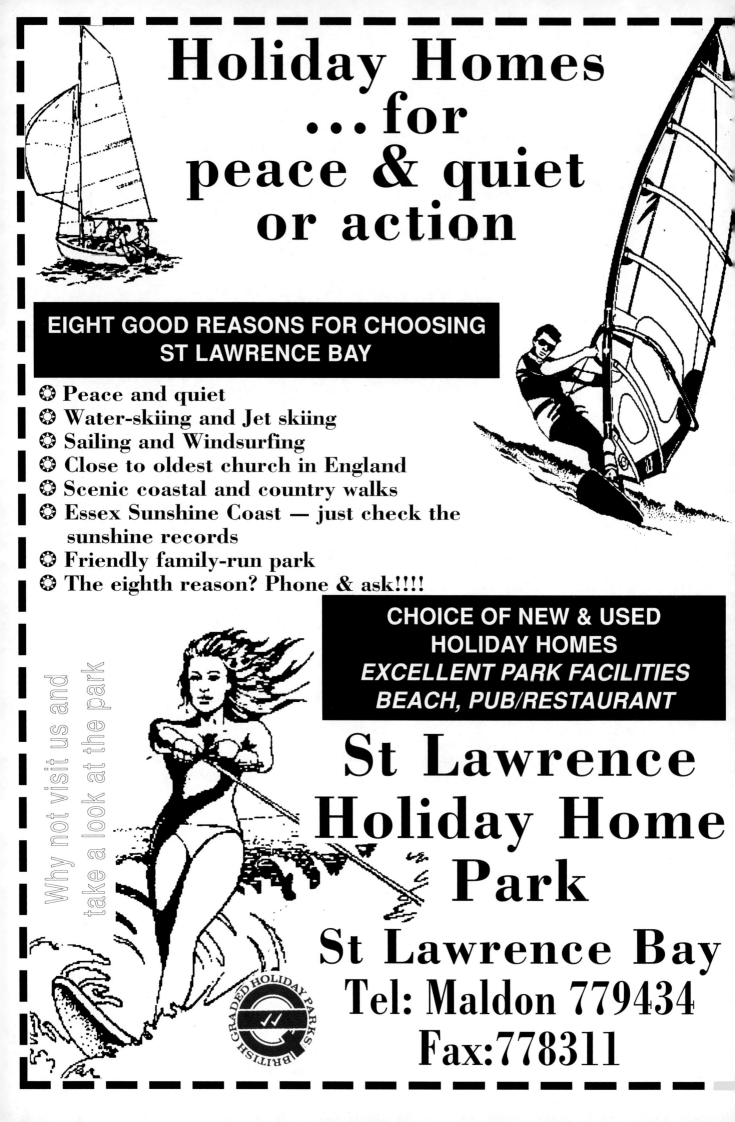

Holiday Homes ...for peace & quiet or action

nurse him through some shaky near-miss heart conditions. But his views on the sanctity of marriage have never altered. "The only woman I ever had outside marriage," he confesses, "was a suffragette. And that was only because she was chained to the railings."

The career of Les Dawson has seen successful TV and radio series, a five-year stint as host of the popular game show 'Blankety-Bank', as well as the host of the show which originally launched him, 'Opportunity Knocks'.

His off-beat and out of tune piano playing ("Now all join in with the chorus") has become part of his routine. And then there are the series of characters that Les has created over the years, all larger than life but still close enough to reality to make us feel just a little uncomfortable.

The Desponds are a family who scrape the bottom of the pit of despair to provide a few laughs for themselves. A small pair of glasses, hair parted in the middle, and an evil leer

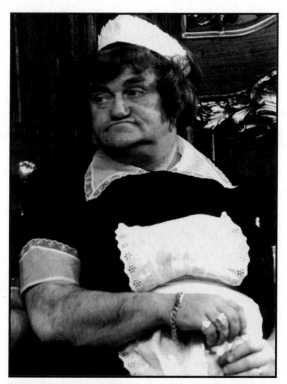

Les as Ada in the 'Ciss & Ada' sketches from the BBC's 'The Les Dawson Show'

make up the character of Cosmo Smallpiece ("Knickers Knackers, Knockers!"), one who Les describes simply as a 'dirty old man'.

Finally, of course, is the perennial gossiping, bosom-heaving, 'Ada', a character lovingly taken and restored from that great Northern variety entertainer, Norman Evans and his 'Over The Garden Wall' sketch. 'Ada has always existed, and still exists in the North of England,' Les says with certainty.

The habit of mouthing the more risque tidbits of gossip derives directly from the time when women worked in the mills and were forced to mouth their messages due to the constant noise coming from the looms. 'Ada' and her confidante 'Cissy' (played by Roy Barraclough, better known as Alec in 'Coronation Street') would have made a perfect double act in the days of the 'halls' and 'variety'. "I went to the pictures the other day, and had to change my seat three times because of nasty men". "You weren't molested were you? "Eventually!"

In England, more than anywhere else, we have always seemed to cherish our comedians long after their passing witness Eric Morcombe, Tommy Cooper, and more recently Frankie Howerd and Benny Hill.

Whether or not the 'alternatives' and the Comedy Store generation of British comics will prove in time to be worthy of cherishing is questionable. Les Dawson's place in our hearts is assured for all time. May it be many a long year before that lip stops curling in disgust, and that woeful expression ceases to register its disdain, and the roof is finally placed on the lavatory.

All pictures provided courtesy of
BBC Picture Library

A DAY IN THE LIFE OF AN AGENT

BY STANLEY DALLAS

Stanley Dallas was founder member of **"The Dallas Boys"** and was with the act from 1956-1974.

During that time the act appeared regularly on all the major television variety shows including numerous appearances on **"Sunday Night at the London Palladium"** for ITV. They also played variety seasons at the Palladium with **Sammy Davis Jr** and **Englebert Humperdink** and also had the honour of appearing on a Royal Command Performance.

In 1989 Stanley came out of retirement, for a couple of days, to rejoin the act to appear with **Cliff Richard** at Wembley Stadium where they re-created the **"Oh Boy Show"**, probably the most exciting pop TV series ever seen on television back in 1959.

On retiring as a performer he formed Dallas Management and has been closely associated with International Artistes Limited for many years.

Among the clients he represents are **The Krankies; Roger de Courcey; Rod Hull & Emu; Shane Richie; Mike Sterling** and **Shahid Malik.**

Buzz-Buzz-Buzz. Not 6.45am already! There I was, still dreaming and meeting a 'better class' of people, as it were, when that damned buzzer alarm brought me back to the real world with a bang. (Well not quite - those were the days).

So, it's out of bed and into the bathroom realising that the face I'm shaving isn't quite the same as the one I used to look at when applying the old Max Factor pancake. Memories are brought into sharp focus by realising that whatever success I may have enjoyed as a performer is now but a proud memory and has long since been superseded by the vicarious thrill that I enjoy through the artistes I now represent.

It's funny how a myriad of thoughts pass through the mind during the course of the morning shave.

'I must check 'XYZ' about the television show ! … I wonder if that cheque has come in for so & so? … I hope 'ABC' doesn't ring today because I still haven't been able to get a decision for him … ' and so on.

Ablutions finished, it's downstairs to a quick breakfast of toast and coffee and away to the station.

Will the train be on time or will there be another of those excuses apologising for the train's delay?

Today we've struck lucky and we are off on the daily 75 minute journey. A few 'good mornings' to the regular travellers - then get out my diary to remind me what must be done today, plus adding any further thoughts that arose during the shaving mirror sequence.

That done, it's time to catch up on my sleep until I hear the 'dulcet' tones of the guard's voice saying, "We are now arriving at St Pancras Station."

Next comes the usual trudge to the underground and, lo and behold, the escalator, which has been out of action for the past four months, is now working.

Into the office, my assistant comes in with a cup of coffee and the mail and we map out the things we must do today and checkup on what progress has ensued from yesterday's meeting.

Now start the phone calls. Someone is asking if 'XYZ' is available. 'How much does he want?' - 'would he take £'X' as that's a bit over my budget?' So I tell him that I'll speak to the artiste and get back to him.

Then it's a fax letter from Singapore regarding one of my acts who are due to appear there in a big Music Festival.

The deal was agreed eight months ago but there are still the details to be checked such as passport and visa information, hotel accommodation, the radio microphones which will be needed, arranging the flights, excess baggage, payment by banker's draft, supplying a drum kit etc, and so it has gone on over the last few months. All these things must be attended to in detail - I will certainly have earned my commission on this contract.

I have just heard that a certain TV company is making a new series so I contact the producer to find out more details about the format of the show. This done, I then suggest certain of our artistes who I feel might be suitable for this particular type of show.

Now I must speak to a major producer of pantomimes who has tentatively booked one of my acts to star in one of his pantomimes next year.

The weekly fee is virtually agreed but we are still negotiating the addition of a percentage of the box office returns, the billing matter, who will write the script, who will direct the show, all of which, in due course, must be accepted by my client before I will be able to conclude the deal.

An agent must always keep his eye open for new talent which he thinks has star potential. My assistant has seen a young comic performing at a small club and she feels that he might have that special something! So I have arranged to see him working next week. If I feel that he does have that indefinable quality we call talent, then

The Dallas Boys (Stanley is front right) with the great Sammy Davis Jr.

it will mean a few years of careful nurturing in the hope that it will reach fruition.

Suddenly there's a panic call from another agent saying that an act, who the agent has booked for a major cabaret tonight, has been taken ill and do we have someone of similar stature who is available.

A quick look through a couple of date sheets shows that one act is available who the agent feels will be a suitable replacement, so we negotiate the fee but I still have to contact the artiste for his consent. Fortunately he answers the telephone and I explain the offer.

"That's a five hour drive!" he says.

"I know that but it's a lot of money and if you leave within the next hour, you'll be able to make it." I answer.

"Okay," he says, "but I'm doing this just for the money!"

Now back to the other agent and tell him that the job is on but that I need a fax letter immediately confirming the deal.

It seems that we haven't received the cheque that I was wondering about whilst shaving. It was due within seven days on completion of the engagement. It's now well overdue so it calls for a strong reminder to the agent in question. He says that it's in the post! (There's another old gag there somewhere!).

A private company, who signed a contract months ago have now written to say they wish to cancel the engagement which is next week. Whilst I sympathise with their reason for wishing to cancel, which is no reflection upon the artiste, I now have to write to tell them that they cannot just write to inform me of their decision and that's the end of it. (It's surprising how many think they can).

I have to explain the ramifications of their action and that they are obliged to pay the artiste in full unless my client will allow me to negotiate a cancellation fee. I can feel that this problem will require several letters before we reach a settlement.

Next comes a meeting with a major television producer to whom I have sent a synopsis of a television idea written by one of my artistes. He thinks that it's an excellent idea and now he's suggesting slight amendments and debating as to which television company he thinks it would be most appealing.

So the first major hurdle has been crossed but there will doubtless be many more to surmount if we are to succeed and get it on the screen.

Well, it's now time for the journey home so it's close the briefcase and away to the underground.

Here we go again - Oxford Circus is temporarily closed because of overcrowding on the platforms. Ten minutes later they open the gates again and I'm on my way to St Pancras Station where - would you you believe it - that escalator, which had taken four months to fix, has gone for a Burton again! It was so much easier being a 'turn'.

Pictures courtesy
of Stanley Dallas.

CREATIVE EVENTS & PROMOTIONS

KEN DODD
BORN TO ENTERTAIN

If there is one matter about which the general public and the arts community agree, it is that Ken Dodd is the great British comic genius. I emphasise "British" because one cannot imagine the Americans, for instance, getting, as they say, "to first base" with his brand of humour. As for Europeans, even if they speak good English, as so many of them do, they would have to be steeped in centuries of British comedy tradition to fully understand him.

Not that Ken is not visually funny. Even if one had neither seen nor heard of him before, it is apparent that he is a comedian as soon as he walks on stage. These days he is not so inclined to wear the eccentric tail suit, often preferring the well-tailored look, but one sight of the raised eyebrows, the upright hair, the protruding teeth and the ever-present "tickling stick" is enough to show that this man is in the business of making you laugh.

He has been at it for nearly 40 years now, ever since he made his professional debut at the Empire, Nottingham in 1954 - over 50 if you include his childhood comic activities. For this is a man who was born to entertain, who started when his parents bought him a Punch and Judy show with which he used to amuse other kids in his own back garden. His father, a coal merchant by trade, was a music hall enthusiast, had appeared on the stage himself and played in a local band. So Ken took naturally to the business with family encouragement.

When he was ten he was given a ventriloquist's doll for Christmas and quickly learned to throw his voice, a useful skill for somebody who even then was never happier than when he was making people laugh. Throughout his childhood he appeared constantly in every type of show open to him - talent contests, school concerts, fetes and charity concerts.

All the same, when he left school he did not immediately take the plunge into show business full-time, instead joining his father in what had become quite a successful business, with haulage added to coal. But he still continued to entertain, this time for money, as a comedy ventriloquist who could also sing.

Always blessed with a keen sense of the ridiculous, he began to bill himself as Professor Yaffle Chuckabutty - Operatic Tenor and Sausage Knotter, a precursor of the occupations that would also take him to the jam-butty mines, the snuff quarry and the broken biscuit repair works.

Branching out into his own business, he converted an old furniture van into a mobile store which he took round the Liverpool housing estates selling household goods, some of which, like liquid soap and disinfectant, he made up himself and sold under his own brand name, Kaydee.

"It was going round door to door that really put me in touch with the people and found out what made them laugh," he says. "Make no mistake, I was good at it and made a good living. Mums with young kids, grannies, men on the dole, I made them all laugh, and in a way that didn't give offence. That's one of my secrets, I think, not to offend anybody. I don't go in for things like politics or religion, except in a humourous way. Everything's ridiculous if you go about it in the right way. But I wouldn't challenge anything in which people really believe."

But his success in the clubs made him yearn for bigger things and, under the aegis of agent Dave Forrester, who looked after his affairs until he died a few years ago in his late eighties, Ken launched himself into variety at Nottingham.

It would be true to say that Ken Dodd was the last great star to owe his success almost entirely to the variety stage. The year after he started, the arrival of commercial television began to sound the death knell for the halls, and Ken found himself playing a dwindling circuit of theatres, though he was soon top of the bill in those that were left and he was in demand for summer seasons and pantomimes which filled most of his year.

"I am a devout believer in theatrical live entertainment," he insists. "The clubs are fine in their way but, let's face it, you're battling for a lot of the time. People go there for a night out and a few drinks and by the time the comic comes on sometimes they couldn't care less.

"The theatre, any theatre, is different though. When people buy their tickets they've come to see the show on stage and

I like to give them value for money. That's why I find it difficult to get off stage when they're still laughing, especially at my singing. How do you just cut them off? I'm still trying to find the answer. But fortunately the manager usually does it for me. I like to ensure too that they don't just have me to look at. I always use a supporting act or two, sometimes more in the bigger theatres, and put in the whole show.

"It's different now than when I started, but what amazes me is the number of theatres there still are in this country. Getting round them all makes it much harder for the artiste, of course, but they are still opening. Sometimes the local council builds new ones, though these are usually multi-purpose these days, sometimes they are converted cinemas opened because the local people actually want a theatre. Occasionally I work in leisure centres that were not built as theatres at all but serve the same purpose. As you know, I have

Above: a picture from "Doddy!" an '81 BBC show. From the BBC's "Ken Dodd's Showbiz", opposite: with his legendary Diddymen and over: delivering the punchline.

vowed to get round all of them that have a capacity of more than 500 or so, even if I have to do two shows a night, and there are still a few left I haven't been to yet."

Because he has travelled the length and breadth of the country for so long - he currently averages around 60,000 miles a year, almost entirely by road - Ken Dodd is probably the greatest expert on humour in the country.

"It's one thing to make people laugh in Liverpool," he says, "but quite another even in Manchester. Soon after I began travelling about I started to compile my own Dodd Dossier of humour, my 'giggle map'. When you think about it, there is no reason why people should laugh at the same things all over the country. The geography has got a lot to do with it and so has the type of town in which you are playing. The Lancashire sense of humour, where they like a spot of healthy vulgarity, is not the same as the Home Counties, where they go for more offbeat humour. It's only in the holiday resorts, where people have gone purely to enjoy themselves, that you find any kind of cohesion, but even then you are likely to find some differences between audiences in Blackpool and Bournemouth."

Throughout his career, Ken Dodd has not been tempted, as have many other comedians, to diversify into other fields or even to other countries. Entertaining the British, and more particularly the English public almost seems to be enough for him, although he has worked in Canada, a country that has always given a warm welcome to artistes from this side of the Atlantic.

Those critics that saw it spoke highly of his performance as Malvolio in Twelfth Night at the Royal Court, Liverpool, but he has never been persuaded to try the straight theatre again. "It was hard enough sticking to Shakespeare's script that time," he says.

In 1960 he recorded for the first time - and surprised everywhere by singing, not a comedy number, as was the fashion among Comics and some actors at that period, but a famous old romantic song, 'Love is Like a Violin', proving that he had a fine singing voice. This got to No.2 in the pop charts - and he did even better five years later with 'Tears', which topped the charts for six weeks, displacing his fellow Liverpudlians The Beatles. But its 1965 release was well-timed, as it coincided with a season at the London Palladium which broke all records - a phenomenal 42 weeks. He still sings as part of his act, "but mainly to give myself a breather. It's hard work being a comedian all the time."

He has never made a film, and even his television appearances have been sporadic in recent years, though in the sixties he did have a successful series for the BBC. He has also been on radio quite a lot, but here again the mechanical media fail to capture the sheer genius of his art.

Some comedians switch off as soon as they leave the stage, often coming across as lachrymose and lonely men. But not Doddy. The offstage Dodd, as I have observed on several occasions, is exactly the same as the on stage persona, particularly when he is surrounded by friends and fans. Even after he has done two shows, having made people laugh for perhaps three hours in all, he is still performing for the select few, who are as reluctant to let him leave the gathering as the audience in the theatre.

Sometimes one catches a glimpse of the real Ken Dodd, a serious and loyal man, serious in his approach to his profession, and loyal in a number of ways. Certainly to those who have come to see his show, making sure that they are getting value for money. Loyal to his friends and helpers. Loyal also to the city of his birth and its people. For many years his audiences, unless they came from Liverpool, did not know that there was such a place as Knotty Ash. But there is, and Ken Dodd still lives there, in the house in which he was born, a Georgian farmhouse built in 1740, which once stood surrounded by fields.

If at all possible, he returns there after every show, to the familiar surroundings and his collection of 10,000 books on humour and show business, stacked from floor to ceiling in four rooms.

A few years ago we learned that the old house was also stacked with undeclared money, a symptom, perhaps, both of the chronic insecurity which often afflicts people in show business and of the Northern suspicion of such institutions as banks and stockbrokers. Dodd paid his enormous fine cheerfully, was forgiven and resumed his career without delay. It says much for the esteem in which he is held that his public loved him more than ever because of it. At the time many other comedians were telling, often in a surprisingly affectionate fashion, Ken Dodd jokes. It was not long before he was telling them himself.

Perhaps we revere him so much because, in addition to his talent, he firmly remains a man of the people. Not for him the champagne lifestyle, the visible over-spending. His generosity - and there are many examples of it - is low-key and unpublicised. He was discovered by his audiences, not the media, and it is to his audiences that he belongs.

First picture courtesy of Ken Dodd. Remainder, courtesy of the BBC Photo Library.

YES NO

☐ ☐ Will I spend the majority of my time doing word processing and spreadsheets?

YES NO

☐ ☐ Do I want to avoid complicated and confusing instructions?

YES NO

☐ ☐ Do I want to save hundreds of pounds?

IN THIS IMPORTANT TEST, OUR WORD PROCESSORS OUTPERFORMED PCS.

A quick examination reveals that a Smith Corona word processor offers the best value

for your money. It can tackle almost everything you require from an expensive PC, plus

it includes a range of highly sophisticated features such as MS-DOS® file format

compatibility, a built-in 3.5" disk drive and an ASCII convertor. With a Smith Corona word

processor, you simply can't fail.

SMITH CORONA®
TOMORROW'S TECHNOLOGY
AT YOUR TOUCH®

TOMMY TRINDER

THE PALLADIUM'S RESIDENT COMEDIAN
by JACK SEATON

Jack Seaton's career in variety started aged 12, running errands for the London Palladium (and washing Tommy Trinder's car for sixpence!).

Born in Soho, London, show biz was in his blood almost from birth and from those humble gofer days he has become an established and well respected comedian, a compere, a manager (even booking dates for Tommy Trinder!), and fully fledged entrepreneur with Jester Productions. He was one of the originators of Noel Edmond's "Hit Squad" series in the "Late Late Breakfast Show".

A list of the Societies and Associations he has been involved with would leave no room for the article, but he is on the Executive Committee of the Entertainment Artistes' Benevolent Fund; Chairman of the British Music Hall Society; elected to the SOS Stars Organisation for Spastics (for whom he organised a sell out fundraiser); and was initiated into the Grand Order of Water Rats in 1991.

Jack can easily be described as an all rounder within the business, panto to management, staging shows to stand up comic. Much respected by his colleagues, he gives back as much as he gets from the world of entertainment for which he has a deep, life-long affection. His work with the Ralph Reader Gang Show put him in front of Royalty and he keeps on the tradition, staging a sell out fundraiser Gang Show in 1992.

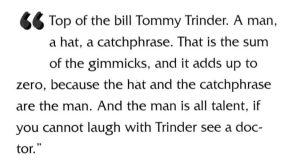 Top of the bill Tommy Trinder. A man, a hat, a catchphrase. That is the sum of the gimmicks, and it adds up to zero, because the hat and the catchphrase are the man. And the man is all talent, if you cannot laugh with Trinder see a doctor."

And so ran the review in the paper at Eastbourne on a show I was presenting in 1983 - and that forty odd years after I first met him and from a young reviewer who had never seen him in his hey-day at the London Palladium. I wonder what he would have written then!

For a sizeable chunk of Tommy Trinder's career, a letter to him, c/o the Palladium, W1, would have found him, associated as he was with one success after another at this premier variety theatre. He was the star of "Happy and Glorious", the revue which opened at the Palladium on October 3rd 1944 and which, when it closed 938 performances later, had provided the theatre with its longest run.

If the Palladium, as it appeared to be throughout the 1940s, was Trinder's second home, it was neither his birthplace nor his birthright. Like all artistes Tommy had, by sheer graft, to scale quite a few rungs on the ladder to fame before he could call himself a West End comedian.

Born at Streatham the son of a tram driver, the family moved to Fulham when his father was transferred to the Hammersmith depot - and became known as the fastest tram driver along the Fulham road!

Tommy at one time went to school in Hatton Garden, Holborn. A week after leaving school at 14 he entered a talent contest at Collins Music Hall, Islington. Mainly by his youthful confidence and cheek he was declared the winner at the finals on Saturday night. Tommy was seen by Will Murray who booked him for his juvenile troupe "Casey's Court". When he departed on tour his mother sewed a five shilling piece in his overcoat for an emergency.

His first stage appearance was at the Central Club, Holborn, when he was paid ten shillings and two and six for an encore. Tommy used to get one of his mates to shout "'core 'core" and split the half-a-crown, one and threepence each.

It was a row over the encore money that encouraged Tommy to leave the clubs and go full time into the variety theatre. As a late teenager he worked under the name of Red Nirt, 'Eccentric Dancer and Comicalities'. He wore bright check trousers, bolero-style jacket and a cheeky bowler - by the way, Red Nirt is Trinder spelt backwards.

The succession of cine-variety and music hall dates which followed were not a great success so, with very little prompting, he left to try his luck in South Africa and in 1930 he celebrated his twenty-first birthday in Johannesburg.

On his return Tommy toured the country's variety theatres, in revue for Jack Sonn and Archie Pitt and as a stand-up comic in cine-variety. By the 1930s cine-variety had moved up market and artistes appeared in the new super cinemas. To give you some idea - for the week 30th April 1933, Tommy appeared at the recently opened Mayfair, Tooting, built at a cost of £100,000 and seating 2,000. Tommy also appeared at the Duchess, Balham, the week of 20th November 1932 and the Windsor Playhouse, the week of 26th March 1933 amongst others.

In 1934, he spent the first of four successive summers in concert party; first at Clacton, then two summers at Brighton, and finally a season at Shanklin, where he became a friend and life long admirer of the opposition comic, Arthur Askey.

By 1935 he was working the number two halls as principal comedian in "West End Scandals" a revue that never got any closer to the West End than the Queens Poplar.

In 1936 he had to drop from headlining to play a better class of hall. These included several Moss Empires on bills generally topped by dance bands: Roy Fox, Lew Stone, and Mrs Jack Hylton - on whose bill at the Kingston Empire, week of May 21st 1936, the press wrote: "Tommy Trinder who follows, is a comedian of irresistible geniality. He has a fund of good gags and stories, and also puts across a number with great success. Tommy also acts as compere throughout, to the undoubted satisfaction of the house."

123

1936 was a good year, he appeared before Royalty for the first time in September at Balmoral Castle, during the ten month reign of Edward VIII. The Duke of York was also there, to whom eight years later, when King George VI, Tommy was presented. Tommy ventured to remind His Majesty of their earlier meeting. "You've climbed very high since then," was the King's response. "Well you haven't done so badly yourself, sir," Tommy replied. The year 1937 saw Tommy working virtually every Moss hall, as well as those of General Theatres: several more than once.

On 26th September 1937 Tommy was made a member of the Grand Order of Water Rats.

Spring found him touring in "Tune Inn", Larry Adler and Max Wall shared headline honours. In the Autumn the show was on the road again with, after very little re-vamping, a new title, "In Town To-night". Thus they were able to play the same halls as they had in the spring. The Autumn tour continued over the Christmas season into 1938.

Later in '38 he tested the water in West End cabaret and was a success at both the Savoy and the Grosvenor House. That Christmas he decided to try his hand at pantomime; in Cinderella, for Emile Littler at Birmingham's Prince of Wales. Elsie and Doris Waters were cast as the Ugly Sisters. Buttons helped Cinderella prepare for the ball until 15th April 1939, the panto's last night!

After a week of rest Tommy worked the Holborn Empire and soon afterwards played some variety dates with Jack Hylton's Band and Syd Walker in "Mr Walker Wants to Know". Syd Walker had made a great hit on radio and became a national figure in the popular radio series "Bandwaggon". It was decided to put a version of "Band Waggon" on the road with its stars Arthur Askey and Richard Murdoch and with Fred Kitchen working the original Walker slot.

Originally, the stage version was intended to occupy only the second half of the bill. On July 3rd the two productions merged for a season at the Palladium, Tommy Trinder coming in with Syd Walker. Tommy now had his feet under the Palladium's table - they would not be there for long, two months later war was declared and every theatre in the land was ordered to close.

The order was not to be in force for long and, when the theatres sorted themselves out with contracts, Tommy - now an undisputed bill-topper - headlined at the Birmingham Hippodrome the week of 9th October, Manchester the following week and Brighton straight after, setting his work pattern for the next few months. Between times he entertained the troops in England.

Naughton and Gold, two of the Crazy Gang, were not available for "Top of the World", due to open at the Palladium on 4th September 1940, so George Black replaced them with Tommy Trinder. Pat Kirkwood was the leading lady. "Top of the World" was a sumptuous production and showed every sign of being a success. This time, however, Tommy could scarcely get his feet under the table before the theatre closed yet again. After just four nights of

"Top of the World", coinciding with some of the worst air raids London would know, the Palladium closed. It would not open again for another six months.

During the short run of "Top of the World" the company had a sweepstake on who would be on stage when the sirens sounded ... Tommy and Pat Kirkwood won it every night as the bombers seemed to run to a strict timetable!

There was no escape from the bombing - Tommy groped from one variety hall to another in blacked-out, provincial towns. The 1940-41 pantomime season was spent at Manchester Opera House, once more playing Buttons for Emile Littler. It managed a five week run, not bad considering performances were given at 2 and 5.30, to allow the theatre to be clear by 9pm.

While in Manchester Tommy was in the thick of a thirteen hour raid. On the night in question he was in the city's Midland Hotel with a galaxy of stars: Sir Malcolm Sargent, Elsie and Doris Waters, Teddy Brown, Leslie Henson, Fred Emney, Joe Loss, Richard Murdoch and Webster Booth.

In his book Webster Booth recalls how Tommy Trinder ran around from 6.30 in the evening until 7.30 the following morning drinking tea and cracking gags ... "All through that frightful night he was the life and soul of the party."

"Gangway", with 4,000 yards of black market curtaining for which George Black was heavily fined, opened at the Palladium on 17th December 1941. It would run for 535 performances and was the first in a succession of revues that would earn Tommy the reputation of being "the Palladium's resident comedian." "Best Bib and Tucker"

(490 performances) and the aforementioned "Happy and Glorious" followed, the latter began its long run on 5th October 1944 and outlasted the war, all achieved with performances at 2.40 and 6.20!

During the war Tommy was placed in the reserved occupation capacity because he was deemed essential to help keep up morale, not only for civilians but troops too. When the curtain came down at the Palladium he went off to entertain troops "somewhere in Britain". On the eve of the D Day landings he was doing just that to an enormous number of troops when a RSM came to him and said "are you the announcer?" Tommy, thinking he meant compere said, "Yes." He was promptly handed a list with all the troop movements for the following day to be announced!!

Trinder took this to the CO and asked if it was correct for him to do this, let alone see it. The officer said it was most certainly not and he would have to give an undertaking not to say a word to a soul - otherwise they would have to lock him up for the next twenty-four hours! Naturally he agreed, but he was probably the first civilian to know about the D Day landings.

Part of his reserved occupation agreement was for Tommy to be in the Home Guard, in which he was promoted to Lieutenant in charge of a gun on Clapham Common. In between runs at the Palladium he played selected dates in the provinces and he gave shows to the troops in North Africa, Sicily, Malta and Burma. He also entertained Royalty at Buckingham Palace and Windsor Castle.

Somehow he also found times to make films, in 1938 a film version of "Almost a Honeymoon" marked his debut. His

wartime efforts included "Laugh it Off" (1940); "Sailors Three" (1941), which included the debut of a young Michael Wilding; the hit, award winning film "The Foreman went to France" (1942).

Gordon Jackson made his debut in this film as Tommy's mate and he later recalled that as a young lad down from Scotland he had no idea who Tommy was and Tommy, being aware of this, kept up the pretence that he was also on special release from work to make a film. Gordon had the shock of his life when taken to the Palladium to see a show, and the star turned out to be Tommy Trinder. Gordon always recalled his friendship with Tommy with great and warm affection.

"Champagne Charlie" (1943) was reckoned to be the best film on Music Hall ever made and co-starred Stanley Holloway. Also in 1943 Tommy made another hit film "The Bells go Down", which played several cinemas in the west-end at the same time.

Whilst the film was showing Tommy was also appearing at the Palladium and, as was his wont went on early to catch the latecomers. One particular afternoon a man came in late, Tommy said "You can always go and see me at the Empire, I die at the end" ... the man replied "No-thanks, I'd rather watch you die here in person!" For once Tommy didn't have a quick retort, but he certainly made up for it during the show and invited the man for tea in his dressing room afterwards.

"Fiddlers Three" in 1944 and later, in the fifties, "Bitter Springs" with Chips Rafferty, in Australia, made up his film roles.

His recording work was spasmodic. The first record was released in 1938 and he

HEAVENS ABOVE.

THIRTY BELOW.

The 900 S Convertible is not afraid of Winter. Built to withstand Sweden's worst, it comes equipped with heated front seats and heated glass rear window.

The hood is constructed with 2 thick layers of Cambria cloth to insulate and dramatically reduce exterior noise.

In the Summer the 900S is equally impressive. Come sunshine, the electrically operated hood folds away into its own compartment providing no obstruction at all to rearward vision. With ample room for 4, the 900 S provides true open top comfort.

Be it Winter or Summer you'll find the 900 S the ideal car for all seasons.

SAAB

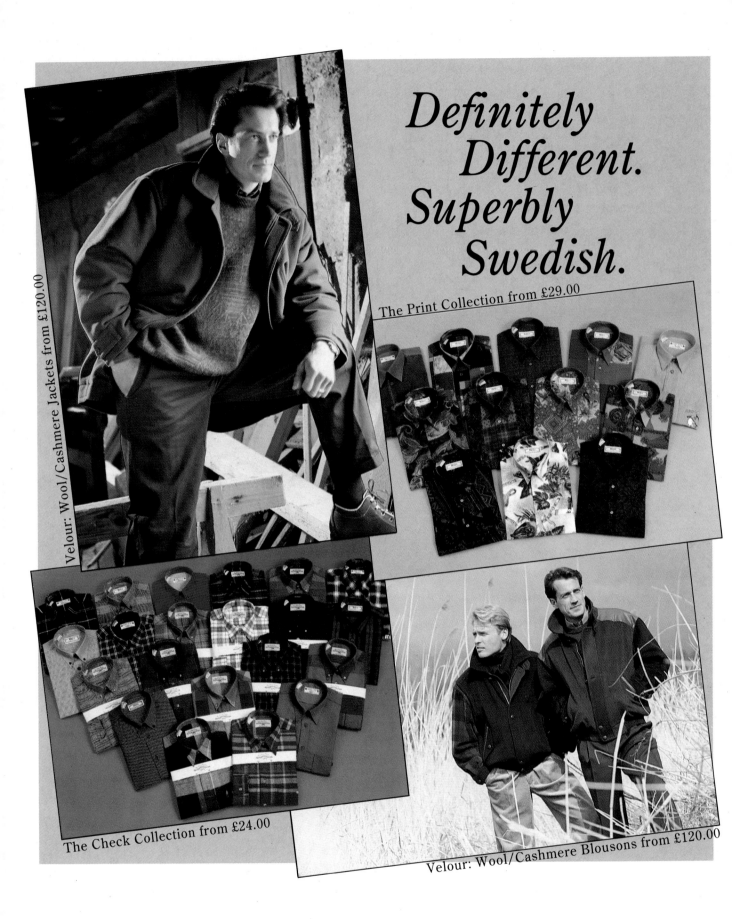

was still making them in the '70s. He appeared in several Royal Variety Performances, the first being in 1945 at the Coliseum and the last in the eighties at the Palladium. Many times he appeared as the 'warm-up' comic as the audience was a trifle starchy in those days, often before the performance started and sometimes with the Crazy Gang, who interrupted from the Royal Box - everyone certainly agreed it lifted the tension.

"Here There and Everywhere" found Tommy again installed in the star's dressing room. This revue opened in 1947 and, in fourteen scenes, purported to relate the various places our hero had visited since the closing of "Happy and Glorious" the year before. The show continued through-out '47, closing early '48 when Tommy undertook a tour of Australia.

He returned to appear in "Cinderella", December 1948, again playing Buttons at the head of a great cast including: Evelyn Laye, Zoe Gail and the Bernard Brothers over from America who, when the complexity of pantomime was explained to them - with men playing dames and girls fellas - exclaimed, "And this is for kids!?!". Tommy was back the following year to play 'Miffins' in "Puss in Boots", having worked South Africa in between pantomimes.

Which reminds me of a luncheon at which Tommy was speaking. It was for the Grand Order of Water Rats to honour HRH Prince Philip. During his speech Tommy apologised to Prince Philip for having to rush away in time to board the boat for South Africa, "Surely you mean a ship," interjected HRH ... "I don't know about that, Sir," replied Tommy, "but the wife caught the boat train this morning."

Tours of Canada and America followed, with a highly successful engagement at the Latin Quarter in New York - during one performance Tommy was surprised to see the audience consisted of ladies, who turned out to be members of the GI Brides' Association. Whilst he was working most of them were crying because he reminded them of home and, for many of them, the last night in England took the form of a visit to the Palladium.

Tommy also toured New Zealand and Australia, which seemed to become his second home and he appeared there well into his seventies. Before we leave the Palladium era let me tell you a couple of anecdotes ...

Once Tommy, on returning to the number one dressing room, had it redecorated and furnished telling George Black, the Guv'nor, that he was in for a long stay and therefore wanted to be comfortable. George Black replied that it looked like a club and all he needed was a 'one-armed bandit'. Tommy immediately had one installed, and who was his best customer? ... Mrs George Black! ...

Tommy, being well established at the Palladium, had a brass plate made for his dressing room door. George Black told him he was a "cocky so and so" when Tommy said he wasn't going to have his name in chalk anymore, especially for a long run. George liked the idea so much he then had brass plates made for each of his star names and presented them to the star at the end of the run. A tradition that carried on for years and they became known as the Palladium Oscars. ...

Tommy, being teetotal, was accused by George Black of not knowing the correct

130

measure of whisky to pour. George bought him a glass with a line etched round, not telling Tommy it was a double! On the night George Black died Tommy broke the Guv'nor's glass and went out to entertain a full house.

Another wheeze Tommy had came from GB's tendency to pop into the theatre quietly through the front of house and stand well back in the Royal Box to check the show. Tommy used to glance slyly to the box whilst working and notice the reflection of the lights on the Guv'nor's glasses and commence to warn everyone, "he's in."

Tommy compered variety bills at the Palladium through the fifties and sixties and was the original compere of "Sunday Night at the Palladium", the fantastic hit TV show which had millions of viewers. On that programme he originated the game show "Beat the Clock" which was brought to this country from the USA by Philip Hindin.

When Tommy appeared in ice-pantomime at Earls Court he decided no-one could dub his voice, so he obtained the UK rights for the American radio mike and became the first person in British Ice Shows to use his own voice.

He had a hit revue, "Fancy Free", at the Prince of Wales Theatre in 1951 which played for a year and reunited him with Pat Kirkwood as his leading lady. Alan and Blanche Lund, the Canadian dancers, also featured strongly with a superb French Vent act, Robert Lamouret - with Dudule the Duck who shaved Robert while he sang 'Figaro'. Sadly Robert died at an early age.

Tours round the UK with the "Trinder Show" and the "Ovaltine Show", return

trips to Australia and another revue in the West End followed. The latter, "United Notions" at the Adelphi Theatre for Jack Hylton featured the French star, Patachou, as his leading lady. The press wrote, "Well mounted and all that a good revue should be", but this one had a short run by Trinder standards.

Tommy Trinder's radio work was formidable and is best remembered for "Does the Team Think?" a show answering questions put by listeners who dared to stand up and ask them! The idea was thought up by Jimmy Edwards and the team generally consisted of Jimmy, Arthur Askey, Cyril Fletcher, Ted Ray and Tommy. Now Ted and Tommy both being great ad-lib merchants generally had most of the show by getting in quick, but did they ever give a straight answer? Did they ever! The show was a huge success and ran for many years.

Tommy was the Chairman of Fulham Football Club for many years and was very proud when they made the Cup Final at Wembley against West Ham. Although they lost he said it was a great day for the club and ninety other teams would have loved to have been there.

At one board meeting Tommy showed his populist roots by stopping the Board from having a fence rebuilt on the river side of the ground, so stopping boys from creeping into the ground for nothing when the tide was out. Tommy said that's how he used to get in when a boy and that they may well be stopping a future chairman of the club! He added that he had had to study the tide-tables because he could only see a match when the tide was out.

At a West End Dinner a sports writer said, in a speech, "The best thing I can say about

131

Fulham is that if the soccer is lousy you can always get a boat out at half-time." Trinder jumped up and interrupted. "And knowing you personally it will be the first time you ever pushed the boat out in your life!"

All the usual round of shows continued. Tommy played several summer seasons in Great Yarmouth for his great friend, Jack Jay. I remember driving into Yarmouth along the Acle Straight - eight miles long and flat as a pancake either side - and getting quite a surprise. On the left side was an old farm cottage with the wall split apart and Tommy, with his impeccable flair for publicity, had had the wall papered in day-glo and written in large letters for all to read was "I've split my sides laughing at Trinder at the Windmill Theatre."

This was surely a follow on from his early days at the Palladium when he discovered that, as he was working on shares, he could charge publicity against his tax. So Tommy took hoardings and had twenty six sites around London proclaiming "If it's laughter your after ... Trinder's the name."

One was in Piccadilly Circus, and one day the contractors informed him of a site at Aldgate Bus Station. Tommy called the Jewish Chronicle and asked them to send a translator round as he'd have the message written in Hebrew. They sent an old boy round and when he asked how much and was told five shillings, Tommy said, "Only five bob?"

"Well," said the old chap "that's what I get in the Police Court as an Interpreter." Tommy gave him a fiver, and the old chap couldn't do enough for him even asking, "Do you have any Jewish friend you wish to write to in Hebrew?" So Tommy wrote to all the agents, in Hebrew!

One could go on writing for pages about this great man of entertainment, probably our finest 'ad-lib' comic, a great career which knew no bounds. He was made King Rat three times, 1955, 1963 and 1965, Holder of the Badge of Merit of the Grand Order of Water Rats and awarded the CBE in 1975 and the personal award of the Monarch, the MVO.

Tommy sent out his own road shows and variety bills giving acts work and quietly remembered others less fortunate. During the war he helped with pilots who suffered extreme burns, taking the girls from the Palladium to East Grinstead once a month to entertain and dance with them, and paying for a box at the theatre every Saturday night for their use. Sir Archibald Macindoe, the surgeon who rebuilt the faces of these heroes, said that Tommy did more to get them back into life than any medicine could do.

We shall always remember his ad-libs and turns of phrase ... one evening in cabaret Orson Welles was sitting 'ringside' holding court after one of his much publicised divorces, when Tommy made his usual bright entrance, "Trinder's the name ... " "why don't you change it?" shouted Welles and Tommy shot back, "Are you proposing?"

A final anecdote ... a young double act on the same bill as Tommy were always arguing so Tommy asked why. One said, "You see, he keeps saying we should sing so and so and I tell him I've been in the business longer than him and I decide." "How long have you been in the business?" "Six months" was the reply, to which Tommy retorted, "Blimey Herschel Henlere's act was longer than that!" Tommy had made the scene funnier than it might have been by choosing someone they had never heard of and getting a laugh from the blank looks that descended onto their faces.

To recall the opening paragraph of this piece: "If you can't laugh with Trinder see a doctor." What an epitaph. We, who were lucky enough to be around during his era were indeed "Lucky People."

Picture of Jack Seaton on first page and picture opposite, courtesy of Jack Seaton. Other pictures, courtesy of BBC Photo Library.

BEN WARRISS –
A LIFE ON THE BOARDS

66 I'm happy, I'm surrounded by people who talk about the business, I'm visited by friends who keep me in touch with the business today, I still feel I'm part of it." So speaks Ben Warriss at 83.

He is now a resident of Brinsworth, the Entertainment Artistes' Benevolent Fund's home. He was admitted there at the beginning of this year after being taken ill just before he was about to begin a pantomime season at Whitchurch, Shropshire.

"I suppose I should have known better than to accept it," he says ruefully. "The fact is that shortly before I had travelled up to Liverpool to do two shows, I had fallen down in the hotel and again on the escalator when I got back to London, which had obviously shaken me up. I had a stroke a few years ago which had affected my left side - a pity because I am naturally, left-handed - but I carried on regardless with acting jobs, pantomime and appearances in variety shows. But I've no regrets. The wonderful thing is that I kept on working for over 20 years since Jimmy and I parted in 1970, and I enjoyed every minute of it."

In all, Ben Warriss was in show business for 70 years and he can still remember almost every date and every incident. He was born in Sheffield in 1909, a few months before his cousin Jimmy Jewel, his partner for 36 years - "We were actually born in the same bed, his mother was my mother's sister."

Ben Warriss when Jewel & Warris were in their heyday.

The family was comfortably off - one of Ben's early memories is going to Brighton for a holiday, accompanied by his parents and a nanny, in the July before World War I broke out, a memory brought back vividly some 60 years later when Ben went back to the town to begin rehearsals for a tour of John Osborne's play "The Entertainer", in which he played Archie Rice's old father.

"My dad was in the army reserve," says Ben. "He left to join his regiment at the beginning of August and we never saw him again until 1919. For a lot of that time we never heard from him at all. He was posted missing, then he was presumed killed in action. After the war we found out that he had escaped to Switzerland and was working in the British Legation in Berne, so we went out to join him and stayed there for two years. He was a gambler, my dad, but a clever one. He really studied the subject and was not often on the losing side."

Young Ben had begun to sing - "I always had a big voice" - when he was a young child. Before he had reached his teens he was Sheffield's very own juvenile star, appearing in concerts and variety shows in South Yorkshire and sometimes further afield. An attack of typhoid fever temporarily put a brake on his thriving career and by the time he had finished his long convalescence his juvenile entertaining days were over. "You could say that when I caught typhoid I was still a boy. By the time I had recovered I was a young man."

Stardom, even on a limited scale, had gone, but then Ben really started to learn the business. "The North was full of theatres in those days," he recalls. "In Sheffield alone we had the two big touring theatres, two No.1 variety theatres and four more on the outskirts. It was in the outskirts that I learned the business, there and in all the other small theatres in Yorkshire, and Lancashire as well.

"A lot of them, I have to admit, were terrible, dirty and badly run with noisy audiences. But by God, they were the places to learn. Fortunately, I could still sing, learned to dance, fed the comics, took part in the concerts, it was an education. And eventually I ended up in the chorus of a big West End show that toured decent No.1 theatres and starred Stanley Lupino and Laddie Cliff."

When that ended Ben decided it was time to tackle London. But in this big pond he found that work was not easy to come by. After several weeks of tramping round the agents offices he went to visit his cousin

Mona Marsh, Jimmy Jewel's sister, an established variety act. Her husband, not a performer himself but well versed in the ways of the business said, "Why don't you do a blackface act? There's a demand for them. You can sing, dance and do a bit of comedy."

"But I've never done blackface," replied Ben. "I've never even been a single act since I was a kid and then I was just a singer."

Nevertheless, he took the advice. "I went down to a second-hand shop somewhere behind the Hippodrome and bought myself a suit for 17 shillings and then found a bowler hat for half a crown in South London. The make-up I already had, and as I had seen plenty of blackface acts working by that time I knew what was required."

Mona Marsh's husband got him a spot at Woolwich Empire, a well-known try-out house of the time, first act after the opening. "I have to say I did well," says Ben. "On the second night I was promoted to next to closing, and an agent came in and asked whether I was free for Aldershot the next week and I did well again, so I was given an eight-week tour of South Wales and then I was away."

On one date at the Palace, Newcastle, Ben met up with Jimmy Jewel again. Being cousins they had been close as children, but Jimmy, then known as Maurice Marsh, had been making his own way in the business, helped in no small way by his father, who had become a well-known Northern comedian, also called Jimmy Jewel, who had progressed to running his own shows. "Jimmy's dad was a real go-getter," recalls Ben, "never content with just being a comic. He had his own scenery and cos-

Pictured during recording of "Jimmy & Ben" for the BBC Light Programme in 1950. Left to right: Jimmy Jewel. Leon Cortez and Ben Warriss.

tumes made, produced his shows and booked his own dates, so young Jimmy had his own training on the spot, as it were. He was a light comedian and dancer in those days, working mainly in his father's shows."

But at Newcastle they found themselves on the same bill and were chatting at band call on the Monday morning when the manager came running in, complaining that the comedy double-act could not appear because of illness. Almost without thinking, Ben said "Jimmy and I can fill in." The manager said, "But you're not comics." "We will be by tonight," replied Ben.

So they went away and picked out all the bits of comedy material they could think of from other people's acts, spent the day rehearsing and went on that night. "I wouldn't say we were particularly good," says Ben, "but we got by and saw the week

out. On the Saturday night we came to the conclusion that we had enjoyed it and worked well together and told ourselves that one day we would do it again."

But it was not to be for another couple of years or so. By this time Ben had almost settled into a pattern of variety dates, summer seasons and pantomime, and so, for that matter, had Jimmy. In the spring of 1934, however, they bumped into each other at the Granville, Walham Green, recalled how well they had worked during that week at Newcastle and decided there and then that when their respective summer commitments were over they would form the double act.

Thus they made their official debut together at the Palace, Walthamstow, in the autumn of 1934 and were an immediate hit. "I suppose you could say that we worked along the traditional lines," says Ben. "I was the wise guy and Jimmy was the fool, but we gradually assumed our own style, rather more than just a comedian and the feed. We had strong personalities of our own. John D. Roberton gave us our first chance in his touring revues, which played the best No.2 dates and sometimes the No.1's. And we got ourselves a very good agent, Ronnie Blackie, who steered us into the top summer shows and pantomimes."

By 1942 they had reached the London Palladium and were stars throughout the rest of the war years. How is it they never got called up? Ben wonders about that as well. "We were certainly young enough and fit enough. But our producers, George Black and Howard and Wyndham, kept applying for deferments as they put us into long seasons and by the time the war ended I suppose the authorities forgot about us. Perhaps they thought we were doing more good as comedians than as soldiers."

For over 20 years they were undoubtedly at the top of the tree as a double act. So much so that they could pick and choose their own work, having first choice of pan-tomimes and summer seasons. Regulars on radio for many years, they were given their own show, 'Up the Pole', in 1948, which ran for several seasons. "Those were good years for radio comedy," Ben recollects. "It was the start of a new era, in which radio got away from variety presentation and into situation comedy. Ours was just one of a lot of shows at that time, 'Ray's a Laugh', 'Educating Archie', 'Take It From Here' and later the Goons, which broke new ground."

Later they moved into television with con-siderable success, working for both the BBC and ITV, but the great days of variety were coming to an end. In 1970, after 36 years together, Jewel and Warriss split up. "There was nothing acrimonious about it," says Ben. "I think we both realised that we had accomplished everything we had set out to do and the business was not the same. We were in our sixties by that time and Jimmy wanted to do some acting, in which he had become very interested, before it was too late. So we agreed to part, though I hadn't the faintest idea of what I wanted to do."

In fact, Ben and his wife Virginia bought a restaurant, the Vineyard, just outside Bath and plunged into a new career. "It was hard work and we enjoyed it and actually made money for the first two or three years. But somehow the novelty of it all wore off, we began to lose interest in it and on the way back from a holiday in the Bahamas we decided to sell it, a sponta-neous and unanimous decision.

"We arrived home, contacted somebody who we knew was interested in taking over and, on the very day we were going to finalise the deal, I got a phone call from Bernard Delfont asking whether I'd like to come back in the business. He was pre-senting the 'Good Old Days' for a season at Blackpool and wondered whether I would be interested in taking over the role of Chairman. Perhaps I might like to come up to London the next day to discuss terms.

"Well, that was just what I needed, but on the way to London I realised I had no idea what to ask. You see, for years Jimmy and I never had to bother about the financial side - that was looked after by Ronnie Blackie. I decided that I might as well ask for £350 a week but could well have accepted less. In Bernie's office I said that of course I was interested and Delfont said that he would leave it to Billy Marsh, who was the agent,

Warriss & Jewel pose for the BBC's camera.

to talk about the terms. So Billy said 'I've got a contract under my blotter with an amount on it. If it's close to what you want then we can do business.' He brought it out and it was exactly the same. So that was how I came back into the profession in 1973."

That was the beginning of nearly 20 totally unexpected bonus years in the profession he loved. Unexpected mainly because for much of that time he found himself a straight actor. "Jimmy had been interested in acting for a long time before we parted, but I never thought it was for me. I had always been a variety performer. When we were in pantomime we were always basically ourselves. But I was never one to resist a challenge. I did quite a lot of variety dates during those last years, but they were chiefly one-nighters in Olde Tyme Music Hall bills in civic halls and the like, for Keith Salberg, sometimes two or three a week. And a lot of the acting I did was in the light entertainment field - I was touring for three years in the stage version of Hi-de-Hi.

"But I found myself enjoying the straight plays I did. I was in a farce by Tom Kempinski at Hampstead Theatre. I did a season at Birmingham Rep in 'The American Clock', by Arthur Miller. And I

was on tour for nearly a year in 'The Entertainer', a natural part for me because it was a music hall artiste. I got on well with the young actors, who I suppose respected me for my years in the business. They took it all very seriously - I shared a dressing room at Birmingham with an actor who insisted on complete silence for half an hour before we went on so that he could get into the part. In variety we just went on and did it. But things are different now, acting is a serious business, to us entertaining was a way of life."

Now separated from his wife, Ben Warriss has no hard feelings. "I more or less looked after myself for several years and might have been doing so now were it not for the stroke and the falls I had which shook up my system. Oddly enough, I never expected to end up in Brinsworth, though as a Water Rat I supported it for many years and my name is on the board in the hall listing the major donors towards the new wing. But it is wonderful to be here, being looked after and talking about the old days. Yet I'm still interested in show business today - I even watch Top of the Pops every week!"

All pictures courtesy of the BBC Photo Library

ARTHUR ASKEY

BY MIKE CRAIG

On January 12th 1978, BBC Light Entertainment Producer Mike Craig added Arthur Askey to an already impressive list of 'greats' who had contributed to his popular radio series 'It's a Funny Business'. In this article Mike recalls the day and Arthur's own memories of a career which was to span nearly seventy years.

It's funny how certain days in a life remain vivid. The day I recorded that programme certainly does. It was a happy day which turned into a very sad day.

I left Manchester on that January morning with the intention of recording Arthur in his dressing room at the Richmond Theatre between the matinee and evening performances of his Panto. I was then going to visit my dear friend, actor Michael Bates who was very ill in hospital.

The recording went well, as one would expect with such a lively Pro as Arthur. He sat there, still dressed as Big Hearted Martha, (all but the wig) and for an hour I milked his memory. I left him at about 6.45pm, settled myself into my car for the drive to the hospital and turned on the seven o'clock news to hear that Michael had died that very day after a long and painful battle with cancer.

I remember stopping the car, stunned at the news. From that day on I can never think of one without thinking of the other.

There'll never be another Big Hearted Arthur. He was quite unique. How many performers can claim to have entertained and become a household name to FOUR generations? Not many, but Arthur could and I for one am glad that I was one of those generations.

He was born in the year of the century so was seventy eight in '78 - as was the Queen Mum, Nat Mills and Sandy Powell he reminded me! He certainly didn't look his age and nobody who knew him could have ever predicted the tragic end which was to overcome him some four years later. In death as in life Arthur displayed great dignity, character and humour.

Show Business started for the young Arthur Askey when he became a choir boy. The possessor of a good treble voice he progressed to be soloist in the Liverpool Cathedral Choir. He told me of an amusing incident which must have 'labelled' him for comedy from the outset.

"You normally entered the choir when someone else's voice broke," he said. "And the lad I followed in was about six feet tall! They never cut down the cassocks, they used to fold them under and put safety pins in. Mine was tucked up so much it felt like a heavy overcoat!"

He went on - "The first time I made my entrance with the choir I caught my foot in the 'tuck' and went head first up the Chancel steps. That was bad enough, but I had in my hand a packet of those tiny little black liquorice throat sweets which my mother had given me. I dropped the box, it burst open

Arthur Askey, family favourite, making one of his 'show stopping' appearances on the BBC's "The Good Old Days" in the early '70s.

and all you could hear behind me was 'crunch ... crunch ... crunch' as the rest of the lads trod on them all the way up the Chancel!"

In 1914 Arthur started a little Concert Party. Tommy Handley (who was in a rival Church Choir) joined him and they put on shows for Old Age pensioners, Church Organisations ... in fact as Arthur said ... "We'd perform for anybody who'd listen to us!" He laughed and went on ... "We were both 'stage struck' but didn't realise it."

During the First World War they would be asked to entertain the wounded soldiers ... "As if they hadn't suffered enough!" quipped Arthur. When they did this, they were given time off school or excused homework if it was an evening show. This naturally appealed

to Arthur who can remember thinking at the time ... "Blimey, there's something in this entertaining lark!"

In 1924 he recalled doing a show at the David Lewis Hostel in Liverpool. It was in fact a Seaman's Mission. Two days later Arthur received a letter from a chap called Charlie Bolt who ran a touring Concert Party at the Olympian Gardens, Rockferry. "Doesn't that sound grand?" Arthur said. I nodded. "It was a tent in a field!" he said.

Charlie Bolt asked Arthur in the letter if he was thinking of taking the job up profession-ally because if he was he could put him in touch with a Concert Party who were at that time looking for a comedian. Arthur wrote asking what they might be offering. The reply came back - "Six pounds ten shillings a week." Arthur was getting two pounds ten a week in the office, so a family conference was called. Mother said "Yes" ... so did Arthur's fiancé, but father made his feelings felt. "You've got a job with a pension, don't be a fool. Look at Tommy Handley! He's in the chorus of 'Maid of the Mountains', you don't want to end up like him!"

Anyway, it was two against one and so he went off to London and joined the show. He said - "They booked me without seeing me. There was a light comedian and a baritone who were married to the pianist and the soubrette, so with me and another fellow, that was the show! We opened at the Electric Theatre in Colchester ... AND THEN HAD THREE WEEKS OUT!!" He went back to Liverpool where his father gloated ... "There you are, what did I tell you?"

Arthur was never one to be put off. He knew what he wanted to do, but with working in the South he soon realised the first thing he HAD to do was lose his Liverpool accent.

"They couldn't understand what I was talking about," he said, "So I 'bettered' myself, as they say, and when I went back to Liverpool they accused me of talking like a cockney!"

If there was a springboard in his life, it was surely the wireless. From a Concert Party comic to the biggest name in the country.

In 1937 the BBC decided to do a 'Coronation Review' featuring all the big names and orchestras. Two comperes were chosen, George Robey and Max Miller. Douglas Furber wrote the show but at rehearsal it was discovered that Max Miller couldn't cope with reading a script. Max threw his hand in and Producer John Watt rang up Arthur. "We're going to throw you in at the deep end," he told him. That was it. Arthur went home with the script and fell about laughing as he read it. Furber had been very fair giving Robey and Miller equal gag lines. Arthur knew it was right up his street.

Unfortunately, when the unknown Arthur Askey turned up for rehearsals, Robey had altered the script and bagged all the funny lines. Arthur said, "I went home so depressed having felt that this was going to be my big break, but my little wife was wonderful. She said, 'Why don't you ad lib. You can ad lib better than anybody.'" And that is precisely what he did.He slipped in the lines and lost George Robey!

The press raved about him and as a direct result he secured the most important role of his life. John Watt called him in and said that the BBC were going to have a go at doing what the Americans were doing, that is broadcast a comedy show which went out at a certain time on a certain night every week, and Arthur was to be the 'resident' comedian. Arthur produced for me a faded cutting from one of the papers of the day. It read ...

NOVEL IDEA. COMEDIAN'S
SERIAL PROGRAM
ARTHUR ASKEY IS THE LUCKY MAN

"An idea, novel in every respect of broadcasting in this country was approved by the BBC Programme Board today. A comedian has been selected and material will be written round him and in the new year he will broadcast every Wednesday night for twelve weeks. Such a contract has never before been given to a radio comedian in this country."

Yes, 'The Band Waggon' was born.

Being called the 'resident' comedian prompted Arthur to suggest he lived on the premises. But first they had to find a foil for Arthur. He said, "Gordon Crier rang me one day and said that he'd seen a show at the Saville Theatre. In the show was a chap who was a contrast to me in every way. He said he was tall, handsome, Oxford and Charterhouse." His name was Dickie Murdoch. He and Arthur met and hit it off right from the start!

The first four shows got a caning by the press. Arthur said, "We weren't happy with the scripts, so Dickie and I went to see John Watt and asked if we could work with Vernon Harris and do the scripts ourselves." "You can do what you like," said Watt, "we're taking it off after six!" They pulled out all the stops and an immediate improvement was noticed.

They were allowed to finish the twelve by which time the show was the talk of the country. 'Big', 'Stinker', Mrs Bagwash and her daughter Nausea, Lewis the goat and Lucy and Basil the pigeons, all living in a flat on top of Broadcasting House! It caught on in a big way. It was even mentioned in Hansard! When war broke out, the Home Secretary, Sir John Simons said in the House ... "We're getting back to normality, 'Band Waggon' comes back on the air next week!" The listeners loved the show. They loved Arthur's catch phrases ... 'Hello Playmates' ... 'Ay thang you' ... and, of course, his signature tune ...

Big Hearted Arthur they call me,
Big Hearted Arthur that's me,
Clean if I'm not very clever,
But only cos I've got to be.
If Mr Foort's organ gets disorganised
Or the nightingale hasn't materialised,
Or the office cat has to be decarbonised,
Big Hearted Arthur they send for,
Big Hearted Arthur, that's me!

The world was his oyster! The power of radio had made him an instant 'Top of the Bill'. (Well he ended up on the coveted front page of 'Radio Fun' didn't he?). Everybody wanted to see what this 'voice' looked like! Arthur admitted to me that he was frightened of going on the Halls, thinking he wasn't broad enough. Up to then his stage experience had been Masonics and the Foll de Rolls. But he adapted. "I was never dirty," he said, "I didn't need to be. I was a Star of the radio and people packed the theatres to see what I looked like." He told me that there was always a gasp when he walked on the stage, which gave him his opening line ... "Hello Playmates, no, you're not being diddled, this is all there is!"

8.15 THE BAND WAGGON

with

The Band Waggoners
Conducted by Phil Cardew

Reginald Foort
at the BBC Theatre Organ

The Jackdaws
Richard Murdoch

and

Arthur Askey

What Do You Think? - 3
A radio problem by Hans W. Priwin

New Voices

Produced by Gordon Crier and Harry S. Pepper

I remember thinking, as I sat rivetted by Arthur's tremendous recall, that I should be doing half a dozen programmes with him and not just the one. I was keen to get him to relate how his 'Silly Little Songs' were born; if his early life in Liverpool had helped him develop his quick sense of humour. On this he said, "People are always asking me why there is so much humour in Liverpool, but to us it's just conversation."

He recalled as a lad walking along Lime Street past the ladies selling fruit. He said, "They would call out ... 'Four a penny lemons, lady. Take me last four and I'll give you five!'"

Arthur had me in stitches when he recalled his Uncle Ned. "Uncle Ned loved reading out of the paper to you. He would say, 'Hey, listen to this,' and he would start to read. Unfortunately Uncle Ned wasn't very well educated so when he came to a long word he couldn't pronounce, he used to say 'Manchester'!" I could just imagine that! "A man was brought to court today accused of ... er ... Manchester ... etc etc ..."

At last I got him onto the songs. "There was a very good comic in Liverpool called Kenneth Blain," he said. "He worked at the Windmill for a time and I met him one day in Leicester Square." The story unfolded. Blain told Arthur that he'd written a little song which he felt would suit Arthur's style and appearance, and he immediately launched into it, in the middle of Leicester Square!

Oh what a glorious thing to be,
A healthy grown up busy busy Bee ...

Arthur said he did the lot, with all the 'Buzz Buzz Buzz' bits in it as well. "I was immediately attracted to it and I asked him how much he wanted for it. Oh, a couple of guineas." said Blaine. "OK," said Arthur, "I'll take it." The song was a huge success so Blaine sent Arthur another, called 'The Moth':

Light and airy, just like a fairy
Chewing up yards of cloth ...

This too was a great success and Arthur knew he was onto a winner. Kenneth Blain sent him more, and Arthur broadcast them whenever he could. Soon the whole country was singing, humming or whistling Arthur's 'Silly Little Songs'. He said that with such a demand it was inevitable that Kenneth would run out of ideas, which he did. "I was sitting on the front at Hastings one day trying to come up with an idea myself for a new Silly Song, suddenly it came to me. A seagull dropped a message right on my shoulder and it got me thinking. In ten minutes I'd written:

Arthur Askey centre stage at the Royal Variety Performance in 1982.

I'm a silly sea gull flying in the sky,
Ever, ever, ever, ever, ever so high.
Two big wings and a large yellow beak,
Feathers on me chassis, oh I do look chic.
Flying very high, flying very low,
You can never catch me, oh dear no.
Happy at the seaside, never having words,
Happier in Soho with the other birds ... etc

Arthur was appearing at the White Rock Pavilion, he rushed back, grabbed the pianist Eric Whitcombe, hummed the tune to him, Eric put it down on manuscript and Arthur went on that night and did it!

With only five minutes to go I realised I had hardly scratched the surface of this lovely man's career. "Do you want to finish on a laugh?" he asked. He went on to tell me that one of his most enjoyable Royal Commands, (he did nine), was the one held outside London at the Opera House, Blackpool. He said the best ad lib of the night was Albert Modley's. "They didn't have a Royal Box at the Opera House," he said, "so they built just one on the Prompt Side wall of the theatre. When Albert came on late in the show, he bowed to the opposite 'empty' wall and said, "Oh 'eck, 'ave they gone 'ome?"!

And that was it. One of the most enjoyable recordings I've ever done, with a man who was a legend in his own lifetime. He had a lovely parting shot. "People often ask me," he said, "how is it you're still working at 78? I tell them, because I'm reliable and cheap!" I suggested we put that up outside the theatre underneath his name. He laughed that laugh with which we are all familiar. I packed away my recorder as he stuck on his ginger wig and touched up his lipstick ready to go out and notch up yet another memorable performance.

Radio Times information Courtesy of Mike Craig & the BBC. Pictures courtesy of BBC Photo Library.

WITH
BEST WISHES
from BUDDY
and
VICTORIA PALACE

THE LONDON PALLADIUM
AND FAMOUS VARIETY THEATRES
AN INTERVIEW WITH LOUIS BENJAMIN

Few people in show business can claim to have been associated with one theatre, and that the greatest of its kind in the world, for nearly all their working life. But one who has is Louis Benjamin, who only recently stepped down from the presidency of Stoll Moss Theatres. The theatre, of course, is the London Palladium, which loomed large in his life from the day when, as a boy of fourteen, he secured a job as office boy, on the recommendation of his sister, at the head office of Moss Empires in Cranbourn Mansions, above what was then the London Hippodrome.

In 1937 the theatrical world was concentrated into a square mile of the City of Westminster and Charing Cross Road could have been called its high street. Dozens of managements and agents jostled for space in the tall office buildings of Charing Cross Road itself and spilled over into the adjacent streets. "I would guess the furthest

away were Harry Foster, in Piccadilly Circus, and Leslie Macdonnell in New Bond Street," says the still sprightly and dapper Benjamin.

Until the outbreak of World War II Benjamin knew all those offices, and the flights of stairs by which they were reached, very well indeed. "My sister worked in the contracts department, which in those days was probably the busiest in the place. Just imagine, Moss Empires had about 25 major theatres - there were three in Birmingham alone - and most of them were presenting variety, with bills of eight and sometimes ten acts, changing every week. That adds up to an awful lot of contracts.

"The big three at Moss Empires in those days were George Black, who was the managing director, with a special responsibility for the Palladium; Val Parnell, the general manager; and Cissie Williams, who was the head of bookings, and a very powerful woman indeed as far as the acts were concerned.

"The Stoll chain, which also had a lot of big theatres but not as many as us, were our chief rivals, but we let office space in Cranbourn Mansions to the Syndicate halls, which ran the Metropolitan, Edgware Road, Chelsea Palace, Brixton Empress, East Ham Palace and Walthamstow Palace. Their office boy was a young man, a bit older than me, called Leslie Grade, but we both had similar duties.

"Every morning, very early, we went round, on foot, to the offices of the various agents, to collect the contracts which had been signed the

night before. Every afternoon, we set off again to deliver contracts for signing. After a while, Leslie and I, though we worked for different companies, did a deal. He went round in the morning and I did the afternoons, allowing him some of the day off. I reckon it was then that he thought about forming his agency."

This went on for a couple of years until the outbreak of war, when Moss Empires evacuated most of their staff to Great Missenden, Bucks - "which was right out in the wilds then" - though the contracts department, including Louis' sister, remained at Cranbourn Mansions. But it was

not long before Louis himself got called up and remained in the Army until the end of the war, with no thoughts of show business.

Yet, in those 18 months or so before he joined the forces, the pattern of Louis Benjamin's future career was set. "As soon as the war began," he says, "Moss Empires suddenly found themselves very short of house managers. So it was decided that I should become a trainee assistant manager. During those months I worked at the Palladium, the London Hippodrome, New Cross Empire - where for some reason I can remember Hutch topping the bill - and Penge Empire, which presented rep. By the time I was eventually called up I was a fully trained assistant manager."

When he was demobbed Benjamin had no particular desire to go back to his old job but, as the rule was that released servicemen had to be offered employment by their former employer, he went along to Moss Empires to find himself almost greeted with open arms and immediately given an assistant manager's job at the Palladium. After a while he was transferred to the Victoria Palace as box office manager - and then came the big break.

Moss Empires bought the independently-owned Winter Gardens, Morecambe, which was a smaller version of the Blackpool complex of the same name, with a funfair, ballroom, catering facilities and theatre, and appointed Louis Benjamin to manage it. "I took it on," he says, "without much knowledge of the North, though I was at Liverpool Empire for a few weeks before I got called up, and no knowledge of the holiday resort business. But although we couldn't really compete with Blackpool, we gave it a run for its money. We didn't do a summer show but eight weeks of big-name variety during the peak period. As an example, I remember one bill that had Alma Cogan as first top, Ken Platt, a popular comic in the North, second top, Peter Cavanagh third, Semprini fourth and, as fifth top, an up-and-coming pair called Morecambe and Wise. Also on the bill was one of the best of all the speciality acts of the time, the Two Pirates, so you can see the quality.

"Funnily enough, the Winter Gardens was never booked by Cissie Williams but by Lew and Leslie Grade, and we put on Sunday concerts as well. In those days, because of the Sunday observance laws, we weren't allowed to have dancers, scenery, make-up or special costumes, so we had to put on a lot of big bands. We

couldn't even use comedians, but we could have a compere, and I remember once booking Terry Thomas as compere and letting him slip in a bit of his impressions act as well, but it was against the law then.

"What's more, the theatre was only licensed for Sunday performances from 7 to 10, so we could only do one show a night. But I asked a friend of mine in the town, a solicitor, whether he could get us an occasional license, giving us half-an-hour more at each end, which he did, so we squeezed two shows in after that. Leslie Grade found it a useful date for breaking journeys for his top-of-the-bill acts between Glasgow and the South, and we paid him £200 for the bill-topper. The supporting acts were booked by a local agent, Bert Loman, who got £50 for the lot.

"I remember that once Leslie phoned up begging me to give a chance to a youngster on one of those Sunday shows. 'I can't do it, Leslie,' I said, 'Bert Loman has spent his fifty quid.' 'The money's not important,' said Leslie, 'give him a fiver.' 'You don't understand, Leslie, I can't do it.' But eventually I gave in and we settled for two quid for two shows and two spots. Do you know who that young man was? Roy Castle - and to this day he remembers when he worked at Morecambe for ten bob a spot."
By the mid-fifties, however, the writing appeared on the wall for Variety, and in 1959 Louis Benjamin switched abruptly to another sector of the entertainment business. Pye Records, begun a few years before, was in serious financial difficulty and was taken over by Lew Grade's ATV company, a major ITV contractor. Moss Empires, also absorbed by ATV, recommended that Louis run the business.

"Pye had some major artistes, like Pet Clark," says Benjamin, "but found it difficult to compete with the majors. But obviously, with ATV involved, it found itself with much more clout because of the exposure it could get on ATV's big variety shows. But it needed something else, so I conceived the idea of the budget compilation. The first was a collection of tracks by our artists, linked by Bruce Forsyth, which we called '20 Hits for a Pound', and from there we launched our highly successful 'Golden Guinea' series."

It is sometimes forgotten that Louis Benjamin, whose name was practically synonymous with the London Palladium until the end of the eighties, had over ten years away from the theatre business entirely. He was occupied exclusively with Pye Records, and also some associated music publishing companies, notably Welbeck Music, until 1970, when he was invited to become managing director of Moss Empires, running this major business in tandem with Pye Records for a further ten years.

He does not deny that the seventies were not a happy time. "In 1970, when I took over at Moss, the company was reduced to only seven theatres, the Palladium, the Victoria Palace and five provincial theatres at Bristol, Birmingham, Nottingham, Manchester and Liverpool. It is my proud boast that during my time at Moss I never closed a theatre. Over a period of time all those provincial theatres were handed over to new managements, some private, some to trusts or other organisations set up with local authority involvement. It was a transitionary period during which the regional theatres sorted themselves out and laid the foundations for what has become their present success.

"But although most of these theatres had been associated with Variety, they are all very different today. I would go as far as to say that the only theatre in the world today that has a link with variety, however tenuous, is the London Palladium. This had some very dodgy years during the seventies, and it was not until the decision was taken to make it available for musicals that its fortunes revived. Now it is phenomenally successful again, but I, and hundreds of the artistes who have played there, regard it as a theatre that was built for variety and has an atmosphere all its own. Despite its size, its secret is its shape and intimacy. And if variety should ever come back, the Palladium is the logical place for it."

The plush interior of the London Palladium pictured just before a performance of "Singin' in the Rain".

Why could not even the Palladium make Variety succeed?

"I think it was because the public got tired of seeing the big stars come on and just sing their numbers for an hour and go off," Louis Benjamin opined. "Suddenly the Americans began to give us a Las Vegas type of entertainment. I remember that Debbie Reynolds was the first we brought over. She had her own dancers, singers and settings and gave a complete show, though there was often a curtain-raiser act, usually a comedian, who did 30 minutes. This set a new style, and we brought in people like Liberace, who built a show round his own talents. But there were not enough of them to go round, and the best open on that basis.

"I think we have to accept that Variety as were in such demand in the States, so we couldn't keep a theatre like the Palladium we knew it is dead. What has replaced it is a series of entertainments. You can put shows on which are virtually nothing more than elderly singers or even songwriters just going through their old numbers, and that, in my opinion, is pure nostalgia - nothing wrong with that. And you can have young performers, mainly comedians, who talk for two hours, with no costumes, no scenery, no make-up. There's nothing wrong with that either, it's simply that they are appealing to a different type of audience.

"We had no need for marketing when I began in the business. A man and his wife would have seats F15 and 16 for the first house on Tuesday night at Finsbury Park Empire and they would sit in them every week come hell or high water. They didn't even know what they were going to see until they got there. Now they have to know in advance and make plans, and it has to be something special to get them out of the house at all, because they have television and video. Fifty years ago, and even 20 years ago, theatres used to do a lot of 'doors' business, with

Louis Benjamin and her Majesty Queen Elizabeth at a Royal Variety Performance.

virtually no advance bookings. Now seat prices in some instances are up to £30 and you have to pay a booking fee so that you can have the privilege of sitting in a £27.50 seat, which in my opinion penalises the public."

From 1982 until he resigned, Louis Benjamin found himself running the largest group of West End theatres, in what was, until the recession began, something of a boom period. Will the good times ever come back ? "Yes, of course the West End will survive. But I believe that the number of theatres will be slimmed down, because I am afraid there has been too much greed and lack of discipline."

But for a man who spent over 50 years in the business and organised, it must not be forgotten, several Royal Variety Performances, Louis Benjamin is far from resentful. "Of course the business as I knew it up to the fifties has gone," he says, "but don't forget that the theatre and show business has a wonderful capacity to adapt to change, and has been adapting for centuries."

All pictures courtesy of
Alan Whitehead,
the Palladium,
London.

A LIFE IN THE CIRCUS
BY KAY SMART
OF BILLY SMART'S CIRCUS

I have been a 'theatrical' all my life, starting out on the Halls (or the Boards, as we called the business then) and later joining the circus.

A great life, I must say. I loved the train calls; I changed more times at Crewe than I can remember. And spent plenty of Monday mornings sitting with my dad and brother in the Express Dairy in Charing Cross Road waiting for an agent to pop his head round the corner asking for a speciality act because somebody had fallen out for a booking.

The Second World War years were a bit hairy but exciting for those of us in the trade. There were so many theatres up and down the country and we played the lot, from good ones to dumps. Just after the war, when I was 17 and working as a trapeze artiste, I met my husband, Ronnie Smart. He was so in love with me that he didn't like the idea of my having such a dangerous profession. So, what did he do? He persuaded me to lie in the circus ring

Kay Smart at work in the Big Top.

while a four-ton elephant stepped delicately over me and then put its foot on my face. Now that's love!

But I'd like to tell you how his father, Billy Smart, came to the Circus business because, "not a lot of people know that." The Smarts were not a circus family that went back generations. Ronnie's father Billy began only in 1946 but he had loved animals, and especially horses, ever since he was a child. Billy's father was a furniture remover whose vans were pulled by horses which he kept in stables at the side of his house. So Billy always had the ambition to

own a circus so that he could work with the horses he loved. As time went by, he became a travelling showman, with quite a big set-up and a family to match.

Then one Sunday in 1946 Billy and his wife decided to go for a spin in their Ford Estate car. They came across a circus on the village green and - do you know what? - they bought it! And, do you know what else? I was a trapeze artiste in that very circus.

Billy and his wife went home, called the family together and announced, "Your mother and I have bought a circus." Now they knew nothing about running a circus so Billy employed "experts" (so he thought) to show him how it should be done.

That first season was disastrous. We lost money hand over fist and, to top it all, during what we hoped would be a profitable month's season in King's Park Bournemouth, the Big Top blew down and we had to work, like the Romans did, in the open air for a couple of days.

Ronnie, who I married shortly thereafter, took over the running of the circus. He designed the Big Tops, specified the seating, commissioned the building of the special trucks to carry all our equipment, looked after the lighting, designed special heating units, booked our routes and travelled the world booking artistes. In general, he managed the whole onshularda!

Before long, Billy Smart's Circus was the biggest and best-known in Europe, helped, of course, by television. In the late forties and fifties, television was frowned on by all proprietors of live shows, but Ronnie and his father realised that, like it or not, it was here to stay and that, as the old adage has it, "if you can't beat 'em, join 'em."

Join them we did, winning the Silver Camera Award for the first show to get 20 million viewers. It was great in those earlydays, because everything was live and what you did or said went out as it happened.

One of my jobs during our television programmes was the commentary. I once even
did it from the trapeze! And when I presented the groups of black Friesian horses I
wore a microphone in my dress so that all
the commands given to the animals could
be clearly heard by the viewers.

During these hectic years, Ronnie and I
managed to raise three children, and eventually ordered a luxurious trailer home,
complete with "mod cons" like a shower
and flush toilet.

Schooling for the children was a problem,
though. Boarding school, though we didn't
like the idea, seemed the best solution.

We were wrong, of course. The school
would inform us that, though the bodies of
our children were at school, their minds
were with the circus. They used to plead
not to be sent back to what was to them an
alien world. It was Ronnie's father who
finally made us decide to bring them home.
He said, "if it's not born in them, no
amount of schooling will put it there."

Ronnie's father was right. Back on the
show, going to schools wherever we were,
the children seemed to learn more about
life and, because they were happy, they
absorbed knowledge like sponges.

We thought of the animals as our "other
children" and although they gave us a lot of
problems, they also brought us a lot of
laughs and much, very much, love.

Once, we were even able to help out on an
important national defence matter. When
the first nuclear submarines were being
constructed, a welder working on the fresh
water pipes inside the submarine dropped
the rod off the end of the holder, which

became lodged in a bend in the piping. If it could not be located - it didn't even show up on X-ray - lives were at risk and umpteen millions of pounds of public money would go down the drain.

The first we knew about it was when three very important and worried gentlemen turned up one day at the circus, swore us to secrecy and asked if we knew anybody agile and ingenious, such as an escapologist, who could squeeze through the piping and locate the rod.

As it happened we had with us a three-person aerial act, "The Antarus". One of its members had been an escapologist in his native France. He agreed to try, greased himself from head to foot, and crawled into the piping.

Hours later, after much grunting, groaning and French cursing, he emerged with the welding rod. Though the Frenchman thoroughly enjoyed the exercise, a £300 reward helped soothe his grazed and bruised body.

Everything in the circus world is very real. Nothing and no-one is expendable, the circus needs everything and everybody in it, all shapes and sizes, colours and creeds.

"The show must go on" is not just an empty phrase dropping glibly out of some witty show-biz mouth, but a hard fact. No matter whose favourite uncle died at dawn the show must go on and on and on.

There really are two parts to the circus. We call them "shirt sleeves and spangles". If

you cannot do both you do not fit in and, believe me, fitting in is as important as your particular talent. Circus talent is definitely

not a thing you are born with. The only thing to be born with in the circus is guts and showmanship.

I am most grateful to the powers that be for putting greasepaint on my face, sticking sawdust to my shoes and showering sequins in my hair.

While I've always had the grit and determination to get where I was going, I've never forgotten that I was not going anywhere alone, as no man is an island. Without all the wonderful people who have touched my life, life would have been very dull indeed.

Picture top of first page courtesy of Kay Smart. Others courtesy of David Jamieson, King Pole Magazine which is published by Circus Friends Assoc.

THE BANQUETING HOUSE

FOR A TRULY PRESTIGIOUS OCCASION WHY NOT ENTERTAIN YOUR CLIENTS
IN THE UNIQUE SETTING OF A ROYAL PALACE.

THE BANQUETING HOUSE, IN WHITEHALL, IS CENTRALLY LOCATED AND
SO CONVENIENT FOR BOTH THE CITY AND THE WEST END.

THIS FLEXIBLE VENUE CAN ACCOMMODATE ANYTHING FROM 375 FOR DINNER,
UP TO 400 FOR A CONCERT AND 500 FOR A RECEPTION.

For further information
Phone FIONA THOMPSON on
071-839 7569

BRITISH MUSIC HALL SOCIETY

BY J.O. BLAKE, VICE-PRESIDENT

On a foggy night in December, 1962, the famous Metropolitan Music Hall, Edgware Road, gave its last professional show. Two young men, who had sat enraptured through the performance of Randolph Sutton, walked home lamenting the fact that they had been present at the death of a great British institution. They asked themselves, "Need tonight be the end of Music Hall? There must be others like us who would like to see it preserved."

So Ray Mackender and Gerry Glover inserted advertisements in The Stage, Times and Telegraph, inviting other like-minded people to a meeting at their flat in Great Cumberland Place, near Marble Arch. A dozen of us turned up, to be told that the great impresario

Don Ross had promised to honour us with his presence. Don - whose brainchild was perhaps the greatest music hall show ever, "Thanks for the Memory", - was as good as his word. He not only agreed with our objectives, but suggested a name for the society about to be formed and accepted the presidency.

The British Music Hall Society was formed, and one of its first acts was to put on the world's first exhibition of Music Hall, at the former Macdonald's Music Hall in Hoxton, to mark its centenary. In December 1963

we produced the first cheaply duplicated issue of our quarterly magazine "The Call Boy". We began regular meetings at the Garrick Hotel in 1964 and in December of that year had our first annual dinner at the same venue, where our Patron was Ada Reeve and Herschel Henlere entertained.

Meanwhile, we had held our second exhibition at Macdonald's, where Jimmy Tarbuck, then almost unknown, made an appearance. The Society was also responsible for putting on the first ever programme of films showing famous Music Hall artistes, at the National Film Theatre.

During these early years, with John Huntley as our Chairman, followed by Ellis Ashton, the society grew and we moved to larger and larger premises, our longest run being at the Horseshoe, Tottenham Court Road. We did much good work trying to save theatres threatened with demolition, amassing music hall memorabilia - much of which is now in the Passmore Edwards Museum - organising charity functions at Brinsworth and elsewhere, and supporting shows at Wimbledon Theatre, the City Varieties, Leeds, and various seaside resorts.

In 1974, under the direction of Don Ross, a group of members helped Joe Ging set up the Music Hall Museum at the Sunderland Empire.

157

On 13th November 1979 the society suffered a severe loss in the death of our Vice Chairman and Historian, Bert Ross. Bert had reviewed variety bills for "The Encore" since 1924, and from 1926 until its demise in 1957 was on the staff of "The Performer". During that time he saw 8,500 shows and 45,000 acts. He was described by the famous Hannan Swaffer as "the greatest newspaper variety expert in the world."

British Music Hall Society Chairman, Jack Seaton.

The BMHS had hardly had time to take in the death of the genial octogenarian whose bald pate and smiling countenance had been present at all our meetings, when the death of our President occurred on 6th February 1980.

Don Ross had, since our foundation in 1963, arranged our highly successful monthly meetings and annual dinners. In this onerous work he had been assisted by Life Vice President, Joe Musaire, and by other stalwarts who carried on the good work pending the appointment of Lew Lane as our new President.

Shortly after another change took place, when the venue for our meetings moved to the Notre Dame Theatre, near Leicester Square. The BMHS continued to thrive under its dynamic new president and continued to meet at the new venue until the latter lost its licence and we had to move again.

One notable event for which Lew was responsible was the unveiling of a memorial plaque to Don Ross by Evelyn Laye, a measure of the profession's gratitude to Don for the £1,500 he had raised towards the Brinsworth Building Fund.

In January 1984, Chairman Jack Seaton took over as our show's manager, and the change was closely followed by our move to the Central Conference Centre, London. This move gave the society a venue offering all the facilities necessary for the immaculate presentation of shows. Jack, like his predecessors, brought his own unique contribution to the society's work, for instance the Lunchtime Variety shows which for two seasons he presented at the Palace Theatre in the West End of London and seventeen Sundays at the Theatre Museum, Covent Garden.

On 23rd February 1984, the death took place of Joe Musaire. From our earliest days Joseph Forrest Whiteley, to use his baptismal name, had been a tower of strength to Don Ross, and had been deeply involved in professional charities. But his unique contribution was his inauguration of the World's First Seminar of Music Hall, held annually at Pendley Manor for 17 years, and since Joe's death, at Knuston Hall under the direction of Terry Lomas.

Before passing to more cheerful subjects I must note one more important obituary,

that of our President for the years 1984-5, Ellis Ashton, MBE. Having served the BMHS since its foundation, holding diverse offices, he was, like those other luminaries Don Ross, Bert Ross and Musaire, almost irreplaceable. His successor to the presidency was Louis Benjamin.

It is interesting to note the names of some of the distinguished speakers and artistes who have appeared at our meetings over the years:

Harold Berens, Sir John Betjeman, Douglas Byng, Wyn Calvin, Peter Casson, Charlie Chester, Leslie Crowther, Coco the Clown,

Roy Hudd, elected President of the Society in 1992.

Anton Dolin, Bud Flanagan, Cyril Fletcher, Richard Goolden, Adelaide Hall, Hinge & Bracket, Renee Houston, Frankie Howerd, Jack Hulbert & Cicely Courtneidge, Instant Sunshine, Naomi Jacobs, Jimmy Jewel, Hetty King, Evelyn Laye, Chas McDevitt, Billy Milton Cavan O'Connor, Tessie O'Shea, Bob & Alf Pearson, Donald Peers, Bill Pertwee, Wilfred Pickles, Sandy Powell, Ralph Reader, Ethel Revnell, Cliff Richard,

Lady Robey, Clarkson Rose, Leslie Sarony, Mrs. Shufflewick, Charlie Smithers, Randolph Sutton, Bruce Trent, Joan Turner, Dame Ninette de Valois, Dorothy Ward, Jack Warner, Ben Warriss, Elsie & Doris Waters, Elizabeth Welch, Lord Willis, Georgie Wood, Harry Worth and Mark Wynter.

In addition to its meetings - not only in London but in a number of regional centres like Manchester, Liverpool, Derby and Avon - the society is also responsible for the erection of plaques outside the houses formerly occupied by such famous stars as Gus Elen, Bud Flanagan, George Leybourne, Marie Lloyd, Arthur Lucan (Old Mother Riley), Max Miller and Harry Tate. In the foyer of the King's Theatre, Edinburgh, we commemorated the great Scottish comedian, Sir Harry Lauder.

On 11th September 1988, the BMHS celebrated its Silver Jubilee with a Gala Show at the London Palladium. In aid of the Army Benevolent Fund, the Entertainment Artistes' Benevolent Fund and the Ralph Reader Memorial Fund, the show, produced by Jack Seaton, consisted of 15 star acts, accompanied by a 15 piece orchestra directed by Don Shearman.

At our monthly meeting in September 1992, the society, which so many pessimists had predicted would be a nine days' wonder, celebrated its 29th anniversary, with packed houses enjoying a terrific variety bill headed by our newly elected President, Roy Hudd, and Russ Conway. And so we live up to our motto, dreamed up by our co-founders Ray Mackender and Gerry Glover: "Cherishing the Jewels of the Past and actively supporting the Interests of the Future."

Pictures courtesy of
Jack Seaton & Roy Hudd
respectively.

THE WATER RATS

BY KING RAT BERT WEEDON

We Water Rats are proud to belong to the best-known association of its kind in the world, but we still get people coming up to us and saying "Why are you called the Water Rats, how do you join and what do you do?"

Well, this is my chance to tell you, beginning with its formation, way back in 1889. This was of course in the great days of the Music Hall, many of whose performers lived in South London. It's hard to believe it now but over a century ago it was a common sight to see trotting ponies racing along South London roads, particularly along a straight mile between Thornton Heath and Streatham.

One group of performers had a trotting pony called Magpie which they raced on Sunday mornings, and on this particular day one of the best-known music hall artistes of the time, Joe Elvin, was seated in the buggy driving Magpie back to its stable in the pouring rain.

A bus driver pulled up alongside, looked at the poor bedraggled pony and shouted "Hello Joe, what have you got there?" "A trotter," replied Joe. "Blimey," said the driver, "it looks more like a water rat," a remark which gave Joe the idea of changing the animal's name.

This actually brought more luck, for the Water Rat went on winning races and after one particularly remunerative success, Joe suggested to his pals that they celebrate by taking a boat up-river and having a celebration dinner at the Magpie Hotel at Sunbury-on-Thames.

And it was there that they decided to form a coterie, "Pals of the Water Rat", the birth of the Grand Order of Water Rats. But before that name came about, for a while they were called "The Select Order of Water Rats".

Now, 103 years later, the GOWR can be called the most prestigious show business Order in the world, and believe me it is a great honour for any entertainer to be elected to membership, for it is very exclusive, so exclusive, in fact, that in its entire history only 775 men have been granted membership.

There can never be more than 200 members at any time, and the highest honour of all is to be made King Rat, a position I so proudly hold. It is a great honour to know that one is following in the footsteps of such great names as Dan Leno, Will Hay, Joe Elvin, Will Fyffe, Robb Wilton, Tommy Trinder, Charlie Chester, Ted Ray, Bud Flanagan, Frankie Vaughan, David Nixon, Henry Cooper, Les Dawson, Danny La Rue, Wyn Calvin, David Lodge, Alan Freeman, Davy Kaye, Len Lowe, Charlie Smithers, Dec Cluskey, David Berglas, Joe Church, Philip Hindin, Harry Seltzer, Johnnie Riscoe,

Roy Hudd, Bernard Bresslaw, Ben Warriss, George Elrick and many other star names from earlier in the century.

When the Rats were formed, the Order had three objects - Philanthropy, Conviviality and Good Fellowship - precepts followed by every member throughout its history. Spell "Rats" backward and you have the word "Star". A Water Rat is a vole and this is an anagram of "love". So an Order named after one of the lowest of animals endeavours to live up to the highest ideals of love, charity and good fellowship.

Our meetings, needless to say, are usually alive with laughter, but there has always been charity on the agenda. In 1890, only a year after we were founded, we started a soup kitchen in Lambeth during an exceptionally hard winter. From that small beginning we have been able to raise hundreds of thousands of pounds through the various shows we have put on, all the performers, including the star names, giving their services freely, and it is our proud boast that practically every penny we raise goes straight to helping others. The GOWR has not only been of life-saving assistance to dozens of individuals but has given support to thousands of causes, including the purchase of high-tech equipment for hospitals.

And, of course, we have a particular soft spot for our own. In fact, it was that same Joe Elvin who in 1909 put forward the idea of a home for artistes who had grown old or fallen on hard times, and when it was decided to purchase Brinsworth Joe put £500 of his own money into it. The Water Rats have had a continuing association with Brinsworth ever since and it is very dear to our hearts. To visit Brinsworth is an uplifting experience and the names of hundreds of Rats, all of whom have given help and love to the home, are displayed on its walls.

The position of King Rat can be held only for one year at a time, but we have a Prince Rat and many other offices, and the newest member of our Order is given the title of Baby Rat. Recently this honour fell to none other than Bob Hope, who is in his late eighties - some Baby! Most of our members are British performers, among them Michael Crawford, Max Bygraves, Sir Harry Secombe, Derek Batey, Gorden Kaye, Paul Daniels, John Inman, Arthur English, Pete Murray, Norman Wisdom, Joe Brown, Lonnie Donegan, Bernie Clifton, Robert Earl, Frank Carson, Roger de Courcey and many other star names, and our Companion Rats, not performers as such but distinguished for their work for charity, include three "Royals", HRH the Duke of Edinburgh, the Prince of Wales and Prince Michael of Kent.

Stardom, however, does not confer any special treatment, for part of our ritual says "We do not ask from whence you came, or whether great or small your fame, for nationality and name, when once a Rat are all the same." The great requirement for being a Rat is to be of good repute and a man of charity and good fellowship, and we all wear our emblem of a little gold rat with pride.

This goes also for our few overseas members, who over the years have included Laurel and Hardy, Maurice Chevalier, Sir Charles Chaplin, Peter Lorre, Ben Lyon and Danny Kaye, who have carried our symbol and our message all over the world.

We meet once a fortnight at our headquarters in the Water Rats public house in Grays

Inn Road, invariably a happy occasion with all those comedians present. Before the meetings start the Trustees and the Grand Council discuss all our social and charitable work which enables us to live up to the high ideals set out by our founders.

If I may, I would like to finish with a poem I wrote in which I try to explain what we are about; dedicated to the public whose generosity enables us to carry on our work:

Thank you all for helping us in the work we do
You'll find among the Water Rats a really
friendly crew
There's English and there's Irish, there's Scots
and Welshmen too
There's tall and short, and black and white, and
young and old pros too

There's comics and there's actors, musicians
and dee-jays
There's men who act in womens' clothes, in
pantomimes and plays
There's men who practice magic, and some
who dance or sing
Helping others in an Order which is headed by
a King

There's Companion Rats and Princes and many
famous stars
There are men who can speak without moving
their lips and men who play guitars
We've been around a century or more - that's
quite a long long time
It started with a dozen pros in eighteen eighty
nine

They owned a horse called Magpie and trotting
was its game
But on one rainy afternoon they thought they'd
change its name
For Magpie got so dripping wet and looked ter
ribly forlorn
A man said "It's like a Water Rat", so our Order
was born

Over a hundred years of comics, a hundred
years of songs
A hundred years of giving help to put right all
life's wrongs
A hundred years of music, so we'd like to raise
our hats
And say "Thanks from every one of us - your
pals the Water Rats."

As I said, we Water Rats are obliged to wear our little emblem in our lapels at all times, so if you see a man wearing one go and say "hello" - I know he'll be pleased to meet you. For, as one of our songs says in its last line - "A jolly lot of the fellows are the Water Rats." These words were written long ago but they still hold true today, because the Rats try to spread laughter, love and charity, always.

Picture below:
courtesy of King Rat
Bert Weedon.

THE GRAND ORDER OF LADY RATLINGS

BY DORITA CHESTER, PAST QUEEN RATLING

Our Grand Order of Lady Ratlings is by way of being a baby sister of the Grand Order of Water Rats, being founded 40 years later, in June 1929.

There were seven Founder Members, all wives of Water Rats, and originally it was intended only for wives and daughters of members of the GOWR, but it is now open to all members of the theatrical profession, and not just those in the lighter side of entertainment - we have a few members from the "straight" side.

From those original seven the Order grew, slowly but surely, and even began to prosper against all the odds in those troubled pre-war years. It even continued to grow during the World War II period and regular meetings were held in London, despite the Blitz and later the flying bombs. Now we have nearly 200 in the Order, more in fact than the Water Rats themselves, a real family, because some members have enrolled their own daughters to carry on the good work.

Our main interest, apart from getting together and enjoying ourselves from time to time, is good work, not just for our own members who may be in need but for a range of charities under the umbrella of our Cup of Kindness.

This idea stemmed from Minnie O'Farrell, wife of the greatly loved Variety artiste Talbot O'Farrell, in 1931, and we raise money for the Cup of Kindness from two major events each year - a Spring Party and a Bazaar. We also hold an annual ball, which is in the aid of the Order.

The Bazaar in particular is a big hit with the public, as distinct from the profession, because we rope in everybody we can to lend a hand, including stars from West End shows, who are always willing to sign autographs and to be photographed with their fans.

We have one specific aim, to present a piece of medical equipment to a hospital each year, what is left over we use to assist as many deserving causes as possible.

Our meetings are held once a fortnight and we get the business part over in the first half, detailing plans for the next event, deciding on the charities we want to help and hearing reports about members who may be ill or in need, so we can decide what we can do to assist them. The second part of the meeting is usually, it must be admitted, a laugh and a gossip.

Our most important meeting, carried out in the most democratic fashion possible, is when we elect our officers for the year, and we have quite a list of them - a Queen Ratling of course, but also a First and Second Princess, three Guard Ratlings, a Regalia Ratling and her assistant, Musical

Ratling, Collecting Ratling, Scribe Ratling, President, Secretary and Treasurer of the Cup of Kindness and so on.

Several of our members live in the Lady Ratlings' own flatlet house, Roswyn in Streatham, where they have their own rooms and the benefit of each others' company. The Order gives parties there from time to time throughout the year, and there is a fete during the summer. Sir William Butlin was very interested in Roswyn, and gave us much encourage-ment and support, which is continued by Lady Sheila Butlin.

Among the well-known personalities who are very active members of our Order are Barbara Windsor, Rose-Marie, Ruth Madoc, Carmen Silvera, Wendy Richard, Julie Rogers, Eve Boswell, Stella Starr, Jill Summers, Anna Karen and Lynne Perrie,

as well as many wives of Water Rats whose husbands are stars.

And we have a very distinguished Companion Ratling indeed, in HRH Princess Anne, the Princess Royal.

But we like to think of all our members as stars, in the spirit of our motto "One for all, all for one." We think we are unique and you have to experience the Order to understand it. We are 200 women in a show business sisterhood, sharing our sorrows as well as our joys.

Care, understanding, tolerance and a unit-ed warmth. That sums up the Grand Order of Lady Ratlings.

Picture courtesy of
Past Queen and
Scribe Ratling,
Valerie Garland

Past Officer Ratling, Barbara Windsor, and Past Queen and Scribe Ratling, Valerie Garland, at the Ratling Ball, 1992.

VARIETY GOLFERS
THE VAUDEVILLE GOLFING SOCIETY
BY ALF PEARSON

It is not difficult to discover why golf has always been one of the most popular pastimes among the variety profession.

Playing in a different town every week, or doing a summer season in a resort, variety artistes, who worked only in the evenings, needed something to occupy their days, and what better than a leisurely round at the local golf course, a healthy sport that also brought them in touch with the local community during their brief stay?

So the Vaudeville Golfing Society came into being in 1921, founded by Billy Merson the famous comedian renowned for his song "The Spaniard Who Blighted My Life." It followed the lead of the already established Stage Golfing Society, but in those days the "legitimate" actors sometimes looked down on their variety colleagues, and it was decided that the VGS should be limited to performers from the variety side of the business.

Many of the great stars of the day quickly became members and the list of Past Captains reads like a "Who's Who of Variety" - Will Fyffe, Charles Austin, Billy Bennett, Bud Flanagan, Ted Ray, Ben Warriss, Bob and Alf Pearson, Dickie Henderson, Bruce Forsyth, Sir Harry Secombe, Charlie Chester, Leslie Sarony, Cardew Robinson and George Elrick.

In the early days the Society had affiliations with golf clubs in or near every town and city in the country, and members were given greatly reduced green fees, and quite often the courtesy of the course.

From March to October there were weekly competitions, each carrying a trophy to be held by the winner for one year. A member had to compete on the affiliated course in whichever town he was appearing, and play against the Standard Scratch Score of the course, the best card returned being the winner.

On the outbreak of World War II the society's activities ceased, but were resumed at the beginning of 1946, with Donald Peers as captain, and as variety was still thriving matters carried on as in the pre-war days.

Towards the end of the fifties, however, the decline of variety created consider-

Bob & Alf Pearson. Although Bob Pearson is sadly no longer with us, Alf was kind enough to put these facts together.

The Variety Golfing Society, circa 1950, play against the ladies' Curtis Cup team to raise money to send for their American Tour. This is now a regular fixture. Back L to R: Charlie Drake, Michael Medwin, Dickie Henderson, Ben Warriss, Stinker Murdoch, Eric Sykes, Jimmy Jewel, Bob Pearson, Freddie Mills, Ted Ray, Harry Secombe & Arthur Askey.

able changes in the business, so the VGS expanded its membership, extending its qualification to any person actively engaged in the entertainment business, including television, which brought in a large number of sportsmen in other fields and radio and television sports commentators. Among these were David Coleman, Henry Kelly, Kenneth Wolstenholme, Jimmy Hill, Henry Cooper and Lawrie McMenemy. In addition, a number of musicians and actors enrolled, to make the VGS far more representative of the contemporary entertainment profession, in which many of the pre-war barriers had been broken.

The Vaudeville Golfing Society is a supporter of charity rather than a charity organisation. For example, each year it stages eight or nine matches against golf clubs, followed by an evening concert in which the artistes give their services for a charity nominated by the host club, with all or part of the proceeds generally going to the Entertainment Artistes' Benevolent Fund and its home at Brinsworth. The EABF also benefits from the full page advertisement taken in the programme for the Royal Variety Performance.

The social highspot of the year is the annual dinner at a West End hotel in November, an all-male affair which lingers long in the memories of anybody who attends one. An evening of unbridled merriment and uncensored comedy, it was masterminded for many years by the late Leslie Sarony, who put all his powers of inventiveness at its disposal, and the tradition still carries on, with tickets as greatly in demand as ever for an event in which the speeches are as hilarious as the cabaret.

Don Smoothey, the current secretary, will be happy to give any information about the society. Write him c/o The VGS 55a Sheen Road, Richmond, Surrey TW9 IYH.

Pictures courtesy of
Don Smoothey.

ROYAL VARIETY PERFORMANCE AND TELEVISION

A PERSPECTIVE BY YVONNE LITTLEWOOD

Yvonne Littlewood has worked in BBC Television Light Entertainment from 1947 and since 1960 produced and directed over 600 shows for the Variety Department. In the last 20 years her shows have included four Royal Variety Performances, three Childrens' Royal Variety Performances and in 1990 the compilation of 30 years of the Royal Variety Performance and the Gala in celebration of the 90th Birthday of Her Majesty Queen Elizabeth the Queen Mother.

In 1986 she was awarded the MBE for services to broadcasting.

It was in 1960 when the Royal Variety Performance was first televised - that year the event took place at the Victoria Palace and for the first time television was able to bring this annual glittering occasion to a much wider audience. It took place in the presence of Her Majesty The Queen and His Royal Highness the Duke of Edinburgh - and the relaxed mood of the evening was set when they were greeted on arrival in the foyer by the Crazy Gang dressed as Yeoman of the Guard! The star studded bill also included Liberace, Nat King Cole, Billy Cotton & His Band, Vera Lynn, many comedy and singing stars, choirs, pop groups (well over a hundred featured artistes in all) but the night will probably be best remembered for a show-stopping performance by Sammy Davis Jr.

From that year onwards the show has always been televised and from 1962 shared annually between ITV and the BBC, just as the performance, until 1990, has been alternatively either in the gracious presence of Her Majesty The Queen, or Her Majesty Queen Elizabeth The Queen Mother, both loyal Patrons of the Fund.

In 1990, because of the Celebration Gala in tribute to the Queen Mother's 90th birth-

day, there was no Royal Variety Performance but a compilation of 30 years of highlights, from those shows attended by the Queen Mother, was part of the BBC's Christmas programmes and proved a nostalgic reminder of the incredible array of stars who have appeared in this special show business event.

From those first televised days - Maurice Chevalier with his very personal rendition of "You Must Have Been a Beautiful Baby", Bud Flanagan reporting a VIP car blocking the street outside the theatre and getting the keys thrown down from the Royal Box, Marlene Dietrich, Steptoe & Son outside Buckingham Palace, The Beatles ... Many marvellous moments and legendary artistes have fortunately since then been visually recorded for posterity.

Amongst those from the '70s - Josephine Baker, Bob Hope, Rudolph Nureyev, Duke Ellington, Perry Como, Andy Williams, a very young Freddie Starr leaving the audience calling for more, an even younger Michael Jackson bouncing around as part of The Jackson Five, Mike Yarwood, Shirley Maclaine, Shirley Bassey, the incorrigible Ken Dodd, the hilarious antics of Billy Dainty - artistes from every aspect of show business. Bruce Forsyth reflected on many of these highlights and looked back at himself 30 years ago comparing that 1960 show! Other clips also included two excerpts from the inimitable Frankie Howerd, court jester as he grew to be known, who made classic routines out of his 'last minute invitations to take part'.

Television coverage of a Royal Variety Performance is very much more complex now than twenty years ago. Up until the middle of the '80s the coverage was set up to televise the production already planned by the theatre producers of the event, which in the '60s and '70s was primarily Lord Delfont with Robert Nesbitt, then in '79 Louis Benjamin took over the presentation with Norman Maen producing on his behalf.

Since 1986 the television companies have had the full editorial control of the theme and content, as well as the financing, although of course always working in consultation with the organisers on behalf of the charity. The principal venue for the show has been the London Palladium, but on occasions it has also found its way back and forth to the Victoria Palace, the Prince of Wales Theatre and the Theatre Royal, Drury Lane.

Naturally any show of the scale of a Royal Variety Performance requires considerable planning and major resources. The concept and casting will be worked on for well over six months. Eight to twelve weeks before production the television Producer, Director and key technicians meet with the theatre management to determine the positions for cameras, lighting and sound equipment so that the necessary permission can be obtained from local authorities and the Police, who have responsibility for the area

171

where the large mobile control vehicles, from which all operational equipment is cabled, are parked.

The need for the best camera coverage has to be determined bearing in mind safety regulations and the fact that it must give the least possible disturbance or distraction to the Royal Party and the audience in the auditorium. As cameras cannot keep changing their positions it is not unusual for up to ten to be needed to achieve full coverage of the arrival, the 3 hour performance and the backstage presentations at the end.

The sound engineers have a very difficult job particularly if the orchestra has to be in the pit for say the first half and then move to the stage during the interval. Lighting must be appropriate for the theatre audience but also be adequate for the best television picture quality. In the early days,

before the latest sophisticated camera lens, this was often difficult to achieve.

Normally an acceptable compromise is reached but in 1970 one imponderable occurred when the unique Black Theatre of Prague took part. They were a fascinating puppet/mime act but they worked in 'blacks' with UV lighting which did not 'read' on the cameras. To resolve the problem, the act performed with their stage lighting in the show and then when the theatre emptied, around midnight, the act was set up again using television lighting, recorded and then edited into the final tape.

The theatre's own technical staff, who know their own house intimately, are augmented by television personnel. In earlier years, the television camera unit was moved into the theatre overnight (after the Saturday performance) with rehearsals starting on Sunday morning and running very often into the early hours of Monday until everything had been musically and stage rehearsed once - then, on the performance day (by tradition a Monday), the first half would have a rehearsal in the morning and the second half in the afternoon.

Everyone had to vacate the stage and auditorium by five o'clock so that the theatre could be prepared for a 7.30 curtain up. However, in later years the custom has been for more days to be allocated in the theatre - for installing sets, special lighting and for artistes' first rehearsals - ensuring more finesse in the end presentation.

When the star performers are donating their services, as they do of course, producers cannot be too demanding in the rehearsal time prior to getting into the theatre. Often artistes are also filming, or even

Before television, the cast of the 1954 Royal Variety Performance gathered on stage. Left page, H.M. The Queen Elizabeth leaves after the performance.

appearing in other West End shows, so their availability is limited.

The scheduling of how people can fit in rehearsals is always a bit of a nightmare. Some artistes fly in specially from abroad so in these cases rehearsals have to be limited to the penultimate or even performance day only. The show on the night is in truth the only time the whole production comes together in one continuous run!

A very large production team of specialist people is needed for major shows such as these and the careful planning, basic rehearsing and administrative co-ordination of the format of the show in advance is very essential - this way, on the night each one, from the most senior to the lowliest, knows how to ensure their contribution runs smoothly but at the same time keep-

ing alert and ready to respond immediately to any eventuality. Even though viewers may see the transmission 5 - 6 days later obviously 'retakes' are out!!

It goes without saying that for galas of this sort nobody wants the responsibility for the dressing room allocation (!) but it is amazing what camaraderie you find when nine or ten stars have to share a room normally expected to take one principal - the logistics are for anything up to 50 (or more) featured principals, 12 - 16 dancers, chorus singers, two or more companies of performers from other West End shows, a choir, orchestra of not less than 30, several conductors and often 'surprise guests'. It is not unusual for some artistes to have to be housed in nearby hotels for changing purposes and ferried to and from the theatre. Wardrobe and make-up also have to be

173

accommodated and the make-up is a mathematical jigsaw in itself.

In the 1986 performance at Drury Lane there was no room for the 250 members of the Huddersfield Choral Society on stage so they were set-up in the Rotunda and the adjacent staircases, televised from there and later made an impressive entrance down all the aisles of the auditorium singing along with Vera Lynn in the Finale. Ingenuity has no limits!

Hiding surprise guests, but at the same time rehearsing them for music and staging, requires more ingenious planning.

Usually their scheduling is done under a fictitious name and they are only revealed to relatively few members of the production team and orchestra at the point when all press and photographers have left the theatre after the afternoon run-through. The impact of Mary Martin's appearance in

1980 when she joined her son, Larry Hagman alias JR, on stage after he'd 'dried' in his number, then later her special interpretation of "The Way You Look Tonight" affectionately dedicated to the Queen Mother celebrating her 80th birthday ...

Torville and Dean's walk on stage in 1984 when everyone had just seen them skating from Australia, were so effective, moving and well worth every moment of the complicated and devious (!) organisation they entailed. Gracie Fields singing "Sally" in 1978 (by then rarely seen here), Dame Edna Everage appearing in the Royal Box in 1984 when everyone thought the tymp roll signalled the arrival of the Royal Party, a flunkey (alias Ronnie Barker) presenting the Queen Mother with her souvenir programme in '86 when the theme was 50 years of BBC Television, the "Only Fools and Horses" scene from the same show and, going back a bit further, James Cagney and Pat O'Brien walking on stage to join

Above: LWT's host of stars applaud the Royal Party. Top right: variety from the BBC's show.

the rest of the cast saluting the Queen Mother in her birthday show.

It is always invidious to pick out isolated shows, because so many have included many memorable moments, but that 1980 year did have a most amazing vintage line-up of artistes - from both here (to mention just Arthur Askey, Stanley Holloway and Chesney Allen) and Hollywood - which in the second half alone boasted Lillian Gish (another surprise!), Henry Mancini, Peggy Lee, Victor Borge, Sammy Davis Jr., Aretha Franklin, Danny Kaye, as well as Larry Hagman and Mary Martin as mentioned.

Such a wealth of talent can cause a tiiming headache or two. Even in the theatre, while the desire is to conceive a cast to give the Royal Guest of Honour and her party the utmost pleasure and to give the audience present their money's worth', it is also necessary not to have the show run too long - but - further complications also arise if the television transmission is limited to a set time and 'gone to press'!

The producer wants to save every frame but it can present difficulties when some artistes overrun their allotted time - and there have been one or two notorious culprits in this area! They are usually the comics or comedians who naturally are best when they are ad libbing and once they get into the swing of things with an appreciative audience there's no knowing how long they'll do - despite all the promises!! But whatever the price, every effort is made to avoid losing a whole act particularly when they have so generously donated their services to charity.

Much planning goes into the security and transporting of artistes from near and far - plus accommodation reservations for overseas visitors - and there is always a sigh of relief when we know they are here and have not missed the flight or been diverted because of bad weather.

Many international companies of opera, stage and film have, over the years, been extremely helpful in re-scheduling their

plans in order to release stars for a day or two so that they can accept the invitation which is considered to be a great honour. For the 90th Birthday Gala the Salzburg Festival authorities, the opera's Producer, John Schlesinge,r and Maestro Sir Georg Solti rearranged their rehearsals so the Placido Domingo could fly in for the day to join our complement of stars.

On the day catering is organised for those in the final rehearsals who do not have time to leave the theatre (and would also probably raise an eyebrow or two if they turned up in the local restaurants in full costume and make-up) - and performance day is a very long one - with many concerned having to arrive early and not able to leave the theatre before midnight. Even during routine coffee, lunch and tea breaks the producer, television director, stage director, choreographers, conductors and key technicians are endlessly catching up with last minute stage refinements and artists' notes.

This show business event of the year takes much energy, enthusiasm and sheer hard work from all concerned, both in front of and behind the cameras, (and despite all the planning I am sure most who have been involved will recall one or two hairy (!) moments). But, when you get to the night with adrenelin pumping at full speed, the overture starts up, the Royal car is seen arriving, the buzz is truly exhilarating and I am sure everyone feels especially privileged to be able to be part of such a very important occasion.

This year will start a new era with a new venue, the Dominion Theatre, and for the first time the Royal Variety Performance will be graced by the official presence of their Royal Highnesses, the Prince and Princess of Wales. I am sure, in the true tradition of the past, it will be a most exciting, entertaining and glamorous night, not only in the theatre but, through television, for the many millions of viewers who will be able to share in it too.

From the BBC's '82 show: Top, a traditional variety line-up; Above, Forsyth & Dainty raise a laugh.

Pictures page171-173 courtesy of Alan Whitehead, London Palladium; page 174 courtesy of LWT Press Stills; pages 175-176 courtesy of BBC Photo Library